The
SHERLOCK
HOLMES
Puzzle Collection
THE LOST CASES

THIS IS A SEVENOAKS BOOK

Published by Carlton Books Ltd
20 Mortimer Street
London W1T 3JW

A CIP catalogue for this book is available from the British Library.

ISBN 978-1-78177-401-4

Project editor: Matt Lowing
Text and puzzles: Tim Dedopulos
Design manager: Stephen Cary
Picture research: Steve Behan
Puzzle checker: Richard Cater
Production: Lisa French

The publishers would like to thank Mary Evans Picture Library for their
kindpermission to reproduce the pictures in this book which appear on
the following pages:

10, 14, 16, 23, 27, 30, 40, 41, 43, 44, 49, 54, 55, 57, 59, 60, 61, 62, 63,
64, 65, 66, 70, 74, 75, 76, 79, 83, 84, 85, 86, 89, 90, 92, 94, 96, 97, 99,
100. 101, 106, 107, 108, 109, 110, 113, 115, 117, 120, 122, 123, 124, 126,
127, 128, 129, 130, 136, 137, 138, 139, 140, 141, 145, 151, 153, 154, 155,
158, 159, 160, 161, 162, 163, 164, 168, 171, 176, 178, 207, 210, 213, 217,
218, 221, 223, 227, 230, 233, 235, 238, 245, 248, 250, 258, 263, 264, 267,
275 & 277

Every effort has been made to acknowledge correctly and contact the
sourceand/or copyright holder of each picture and Carlton Books Limited
apologizesfor any unintentional errors or omissions, which will be corrected
in future editions of this book.

Printed in China

The SHERLOCK HOLMES

Puzzle Collection

THE LOST CASES

Dr John Watson

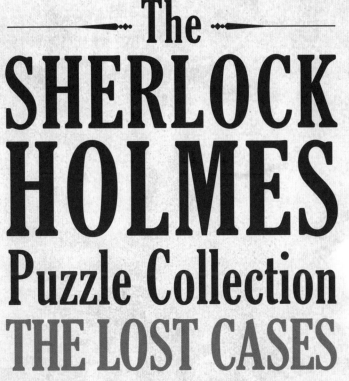

Over 140 cerebral
challenges, inspired by the
world's greatest detective

SEVENOAKS

CONTENTS

Introduction   8

ELEMENTARY

On The Strand	12	170	Scarves	31	175
Granddad	13	170	Joe	32	175
Spheres	14	170	The Wenns	33	176
Hookland	15	171	Maida Vale	34	176
The Watchmen	16	171	Sheep	35	176
The Prison	17	171	The Second Wordknot	36	176
The First Wordknot	18	171	The Partner	37	177
Whisky	19	172	Fruity	38	177
Cousin Tracy	20	172	Hands	39	177
Passing By	21	172	Cider	40	178
The Candles	22	173	A Sense Of Urgency	42	178
Trilogy	24	173	Hot and Cold	43	178
Buckets	25	173	On The Buses	44	178
The Maddened Miller	26	173	Hookland Knights	45	179
The First Camouflage	27	173	The Third Wordknot	46	179
Fabulous	28	174	The Painting	47	179
Out East	29	174	Daniel	48	179
The Suicide	30	175			

STRAIGHTFORWARD

The Pleasant Lake	52	182	Dangerous Ladies	69	187
The Uncle	53	182	Square Sheep	70	188
Slick	54	182	Mr Andreas	71	188
The Second Camouflage	54	182	The Bottle	72	189
Forty-Five	55	183	Davey	73	189
St Mary Axe	56	183	The Watch	74	189
Great-Aunt Ada	57	183	The Fifth Wordknot	75	189
Ronnie	58	184	The Lease	76	190
February	58	184	Tea	77	190
Isaac	59	184	Loose Change	78	190
The Code	60	185	How Many Cows	80	191
The Track	61	185	Odd	81	191
A Chelsea Tale	62	186	Draft	82	192
Express	64	186	The Seamstress	83	192
The Fence	65	186	Bees	84	193
The Fourth Wordknot	66	187	Fruitful	85	193
The One	67	187	The Third Camouflage	86	193
The Biscuits	68	187	Speed	87	193

CUNNING

The Weights	90	196
Solaris	91	196
A Worship of Writers	92	197
Loggers	94	197
The Sixth Wordknot	95	197
Two Sums	96	197
Duck Duck Goose	98	198
The Jeweller	99	198
The Note	100	198
Serpentine	101	198
The Legacy	102	199
Children	103	199
The Revenge	104	199
The Trunk	106	200
The Field	107	200
The Type	108	201
Stabbing	109	201
Balance	110	201
The Manager	111	202
Getting Ahead	112	202
Bicycle	113	203
The Canvas	114	203
Pig	115	204
The Seventh Wordknot	116	205
The Shopkeeper	117	205
Match Two	118	205
Curio	119	206
Six Feet Under	120	206
Engine Trouble	121	207
Recall	122	207
Moran	123	208
The Eighth Wordknot	124	208
Barnabas	125	208
The Forty-Four	126	209
The Murder of Molly Glass	127	209

FIENDISH

Pipe Dreams	130	212	The Enthusiast	148	218
The Old Ones	131	212	The Fifth Camouflage	150	218
Rifle Rounds	132	213	The Ribbons	151	219
The Pleasant Way	133	213	Billy and Jonny	152	219
Fashion	134	213	Trout	153	219
The Fourth Camouflage	135	214	Getting To Market	154	220
The Apple Market	136	214	The Tenth Wordknot	156	220
A Pair of Fours	137	214	Pencils	157	220
Ashcourt Station	138	215	Two Wrongs	158	221
Andrew	139	215	Easter Spirit	159	221
Centurial	140	215	Three Men	160	222
Rock Paper Scissors	141	216	Rufus	162	222
Old Hook	142	216	Manual	163	223
Art	144	217	The Tyrant	164	223
Daisy	145	217	The Final Camouflage	165	223
The Ninth Wordknot	146	217	Seven Applewomen	166	224
The Seven	147	217	Terminus	167	224
Bridge	147	218			

INTRODUCTION

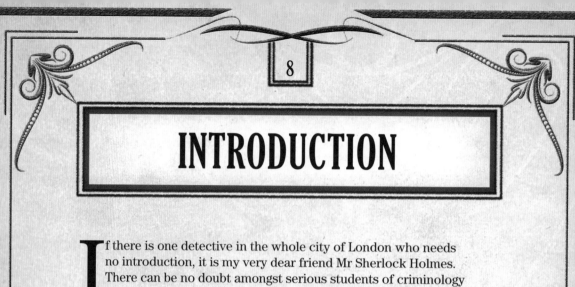

If there is one detective in the whole city of London who needs no introduction, it is my very dear friend Mr Sherlock Holmes. There can be no doubt amongst serious students of criminology that he possesses the finest mind in the whole field. His powers of observation are beyond measure, and his ability to know almost every pertinent detail of a person's life at a single glance is a source of unending awe to any person who has been lucky enough to meet him. But you know all this, of course, since his name is so prominent in both newspapers and more serious analytical literature.

Sadly, I am far less blessed. I have attempted in my way to be of some help to the sick and needy, but my great fortune lies in the dear friendship of that incredible man. I have been privileged enough to share in many of Holmes' adventures as his companion, and to have shared lodgings with him from time to time, and so it has fallen to me to be something of an unofficial biographer of his achievements. You may even have come across one of my accounts of his doings, though I admit the chance is slim.

Holmes's greatest passion is the human facility for logic and deduction. He is quite unselfish in this. He works ceaselessly to better himself, not for his own aggrandizement, but because he devoutly believes that this is the most important work available to humanity as a whole. Likewise, he has long cherished an earnest desire to improve the minds of the masses – starting, in most practical cases, with myself. But time is a scant resource, and there is much villainy forever demanding Holmes's immediate and urgent attention. Which is why I have taken the liberty of assembling this book. As I have alluded, I have often been on the receiving end of mental exercises devised by Holmes to strengthen my facilities for analysis, logic, reason, arithmetic, creative thought and deduction. I have

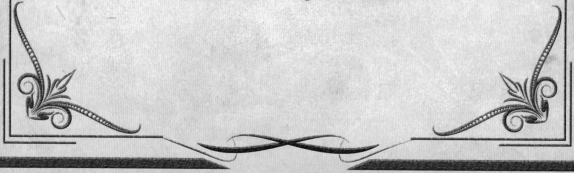

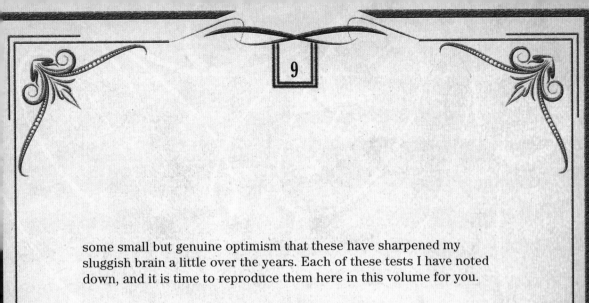

some small but genuine optimism that these have sharpened my sluggish brain a little over the years. Each of these tests I have noted down, and it is time to reproduce them here in this volume for you.

I hope and trust that you will find them diverting, and if even one of them causes you to think about the world in a more analytical manner, I know that Holmes would be satisfied. I take no credit for any of the contents herein; I am a scribe, and nothing more. However, one thing I have attempted to do – with greater or lesser success – is to group the 140 puzzles by their approximate difficulty. This is a haphazard proposition at best. As a wise man once said, "All questions are hard if you don't know the answer, and easy if you do." Undoubtedly, you will find that my categorizations fail you from time to time, and for that I am apologize. I can judge them only by my own poor mind.

My dear friends, it gives me a very great pleasure to present to you this second volume of the puzzles of Mr Sherlock Holmes.

I remain, in all ways, your servant,

Dr John H. Watson,
221b Baker Street, London NW1 6XE

ELEMENTARY PUZZLES

ON THE STRAND

During *The Nasty Affair of the Highwayman's Daughter*, Mr Sherlock Holmes and I found ourselves in a luxurious room on the third floor of a hotel on the Strand. The woman in question — I hesitate to describe her as a lady — was as black-hearted as any I've encountered. We were holed up in Room 303, Holmes cunningly disguised as a Keralan fakir. Our quarry was next door, with some of her next targets. We were preparing to apprehend her when, sadly, events overtook us.

———————◆◆◆———————

There was a shriek from Room 304, and then a woman's voice shouting "No, Hugo! Don't shoot! *No!*" This was followed by a loud gunshot.

We immediately made a dash for 304. The door was unlocked, and we burst in. I'm not ashamed to say that I had my revolver in my hand. Inside, we found a grim scene. The highwayman's daughter lay dead on the floor. At the far end of the room clustered three people, all white-faced, in clear shock. The gun lay at their feet, where it had clearly been dropped by nerveless hands.

Holmes took one look at the group, and said, "Obviously a teacher, a tailor and a lawyer," indicating each in turn. "Watson, restrain the..."

"Lawyer," I said, seizing the unique chance to stick my oar in.

"Clearly," Holmes said, with just the faintest hint of irritation. But how did I of all people know which was the guilty party?

✳ Solution on page 170 ✳

GRANDDAD

You might be interested in this minor follow-up to *The Nasty Affair of the Highwayman's Daughter*. A day later, Holmes and I were back in our lodgings at 221b Baker Street, and I was writing up my notes on the case. Holmes sat there thoughtfully for a period of time, puffing his pipe, whilst I scratched away with my pen.

———◆———

Eventually, he turned to me. "Her father was quite old, you know," he said.

It seemed an odd point for Holmes to make. "Oh?" I replied.

He nodded. "Older than her grandfather, in fact."

"What?"

He arched an eyebrow at my reaction.

Whatever did he mean?

✳ Solution on page 170 ✳

SPHERES

Early on in our relationship, as I have already mentioned elsewhere, Holmes decided that my mental faculties and deductive abilities could be improved by rigorous practice. He took it upon himself to torment me with all manner of conundrums. These were generally presented without warning on the grounds that deduction often had to be called upon under pressure.

I had just sunk into a delightfully hot bath one evening when Holmes's voice floated in to me. "Imagine a ball, Watson."

"Very well," I called back, confident that my quiet sigh had gone unheard.

"Make it a perfect sphere. And don't sigh! Your betterment is the most worthy of causes."

"Indeed," I replied. "So, I have this sphere. What now?"

"Tell me, if you can, what is the probability that any three points chosen at random will fall into a single hemisphere on its surface? You may assume that the dividing line between hemispheres is vanishingly small."

"I shall," I said, and setting relaxation aside, began thinking.

Can you find the solution?

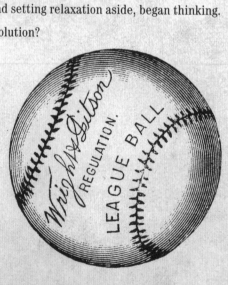

※ Solution on page 170 ※

HOOKLAND

Holmes and I found ourselves in rural Hookland one Tuesday afternoon, some miles east of Coreham, just in sight of Eden Tor. Holmes had taken on the guise of a local farmer, in order to better observe the movements of Major C. L. Nolan. We were standing at a fence, looking over the estates that Nolan was currently visiting, when a genuine local approached us. Holmes turned and leaned back against the fence to watch the newcomer approach, elbows resting behind him on the top strut.

The fellow came to about ten feet away, and stopped.

"Yalreet, boi?" said Holmes conversationally.

"Yalreet," replied the farmer. "Ow's yur mools?"

Holmes scratched his chin thoughtfully. "Li'l buggers is 'ow."

The pair of them continued in this fashion for some time, before the fellow lolloped off again, apparently satisfied as to our bona fides. Once he'd gone, Holmes explained that they'd been talking about moles.

"Our visitor claimed to have caught an entire nest of moles this morning," Holmes told me. "He furthermore suggested that five of them were completely blind in the right eye, four blind in the left, three sighted in the left eye, two sighted in the right, and one sighted in both. I told him the least number of moles that could be, which is when he nodded and left."

"So you weren't discussing Potemkin after all, then?" I muttered.

How many moles did the farmer catch?

❋ Solution on page 171 ❋

THE WATCHMEN

Holmes and I had cause to observe a warehouse near Wapping Docks during the adventure of the frightened carpenter. A rather expensive necklace had been stolen and we had been charged with its safe return. The warehouse was guarded by a pair of rough-looking men with a little sentry post. Every hour on the hour, one of them would start off on a complex route around the grounds, winding in and out of stacks of pallets at a constant pace, returning finally to the post 45 minutes later.

The men took it in turns to make their round, and the route that they took was always the same, but sometimes they progressed in a clockwise manner, heading left from the hut, and sometimes anticlockwise, heading right. This choice appeared to be settled, as far as we could tell, by the toss of a coin.

"If I were going to assault this place," Holmes said, after some hours of observation, "I know when I'd choose. The guard is in the same spot at a specific time every hour. That's when I'd strike."

"How can you possibly know that?" I protested. "You don't know which way the fellow is going to head."

"It's obvious," Holmes said.

How?

✳ Solution on page 171 ✳

THE PRISON

"You are incarcerated, Watson," Holmes told me one morning over my kippers.

———◆———

"I am?"

"Indeed so. In some backwater town in Albania, say."

"How unfortunate," I replied. "Their prison cook seems quite satisfactory, however."

"Luckily for you, the prison warden is a megalomaniac with an obsession for mathematical riddles."

"Sounds all too plausible, old chap."

"You are offered a chance," Holmes continued loftily. "Your door contains a combination lock with five dials, each numbered 0 to 9. You may serve out your time peacefully, or you may tell the guard your guess for how many possible combinations there are for your lock. If your guess is correct within five per cent, you will be set free. If it is wrong, you will be put to death. What do you do?"

What I actually did was eat some more kipper, and ponder permutations. How many combinations do you think there are for the lock?

✳ **Solution on page 171** ✳

THE FIRST WORDKNOT

As I was going through some medical textbooks one afternoon, hoping to confirm a diagnostic suspicion regarding a patient, Holmes accosted me bearing a slip of paper.

"Here," he told me urgently. "Take this."

I glanced at the paper. It bore the following message:

1. CDP
2. EHE
3. LOP
4. PIC
5. ECO
6. ARL
7. MAC
8. ITI
9. EEN
10. TSS

"What is it, Holmes? Some sort of devilish cipher?"

"Not too devilish, I trust," he told me. "There are three ten-letter words on this note. The first line bears their initial letters, the second their second letters, and so on, until the tenth line, which bears their final letters. However, on each line, the three letters are jumbled around. The words are linked by a loose theme. Can you find them?"

The penny dropped. "This is a test?"

"Obviously."

Can you find the three words?

✻ Solution on page 171 ✻

WHISKY

I took a sip from my glass of whisky, and relaxed back into the armchair, enjoying the warmth of the merry fireplace in front of us. "This is excellent, Holmes."

He nodded. "As it should be, at seven shillings."

I winced. "Can you get anything back for the empty bottle?"

"Yes, the whisky is worth 80 pence more than the glass."

There are, of course, twelve pence to the shilling. How much was the bottle worth?

✳ Solution on page 172 ✳

COUSIN TRACY

Having befuddled me with her candle purchases, Mrs Hudson proceeded to recount a lengthy and somewhat muddled story regarding her cousin Tracy, and Tracy's husband Albert. As best I could ascertain, both Tracy and Albert were on their second marriages, having lost their earlier spouses to illness, or possibly misadventure.

Clearly this shared loss proved a bond for the couple. The family now stretched to nine children in total, quite the brood. There was a certain amount of tension between his children, her children, and their children, and their shenanigans appeared to be the foundation of the anecdote.

From what I could glean from the mess of names and dates, Tracy and Albert each had six children whom they could call their own in a biological sense. Mrs Hudson neglected to specify how many had been born from the happy couple's union, and Holmes was quick to inform me that I ought to be able to work it out for myself.

Can you say how many were children of both Tracy and Albert?

* **Solution on page 172** *

PASSING BY

The Adventure of the Wandering Bishops saw Holmes and I on the train from Waterloo to Weychester one Tuesday morning. Our idle conversation was interrupted by a train rattling past loudly on the other track. Once it was clear, Holmes announced that the intruding train had been half our own train's length of 400 feet. I complimented him on his good eye for such things. I rather hoped that might close the matter, but as it transpired, I was wrong.

"I can tell you that it took the two trains just five seconds to pass each other in their entirety. Furthermore, if the two had been travelling in the same direction, the faster would have passed the slower in precisely fifteen seconds."

"Is that so?" I hoped I managed to convey interest.

"Can you tell me what speed the faster of the two trains is running at? Feet per second will do perfectly well as a unit of measurement."

Can you find the solution?

❋ Solution on page 172 ❋

THE CANDLES

"There's something wrong with that new candle-boy," Mrs Hudson observed one morning, when she arrived to remove our breakfast things. "He absolutely refuses to deliver normal-sized boxes of candles."

———————————

Holmes sat up, evidently curious. "How so, Mrs Hudson?"

"He says he's only got six sizes of box, and he's not breaking them for nobody. It wouldn't be so bad if his boxes weren't so stupid."

"Oh?" I asked, now intrigued despite myself.

She nodded, clearly irritated just by the thought of it. "His boxes come in lots of sixteen, seventeen, twenty-three, twenty-four, thirty-nine, and forty candles. That's all. They're all the same size. It's ridiculous. He says I have to make an order for specific amounts of the various boxes."

I smiled at her sympathetically. "And how many candles do you normally order, my dear lady?"

"One hundred," she said. "We go through them like nobody's business. I don't dare order them now, though."

Holmes snorted and sagged back into his chair, which I took to mean the end of his interest in the matter.

Could Mrs Hudson get her candles, and if so, what would she have to order?

TO
LET

TRILOGY

Mrs Hudson's final shot, after well over a quarter of an hour of the most baffling details of her cousin Tracy's extended family, was the strange fate of a loosely-related in-law. Cousin Tracy's husband's brother's cousin-in-law's father, to be precise. This worthy, whose name I didn't catch, had apparently served in the Zulu war of '79. He had been exposed to some horrifying brutalities whilst out there, and on his return, was never quite the same.

Some years later, as Mrs Hudson would have it, the former soldier was at his parish church with wife and child, as was usual on a Sunday. On this ill-fated occasion, he dozen off quietly, falling into a terrible nightmare about being captured by the Zulus with the rest of his brigade. The Zulus began decapitating their prisoners one by one. In the dream, he was about to meet the same fate when his wife, realizing her husband was asleep, tapped him on the back of the neck with her fan to wake him up. The sudden shock overwhelmed his already-stressed system, and he immediately dropped stone dead.

This was the point at which Holmes rose from his seat and politely but forcefully thanked Mrs Hudson for breakfast, and ushered her out of our rooms. Closing the door behind her, Holmes muttered, "Blatant piffle!" He then stalked off in high dudgeon, and moments later the sounds of aggrieved violin-playing filled the air.

Why did Holmes disbelieve Mrs Hudson?

✻ Solution on page 173 ✻

BUCKETS

I was cleaning my pipe one evening, with my revolver shortly to follow, when Holmes appeared in my peripheral vision and placed a big metal bucket in front of me with a loud clang. I startled, turning to look at him as I pulled backwards.

"Water," Holmes declared.

"I'm fine for the moment, thanks," I told him as patiently as I was able.

"You misunderstand," he said.

I nodded glumly. "I dare say I do."

"Two identical buckets, filled to the precise brim with water." He paused. "Pray engage your imagination. This empty one is by way of illustration."

"Done," I said. "Although I dare say I could have managed the feat without a real-world model."

"Reassuring to hear," Holmes said. "Now, one of the buckets has a large chunk of wood floating in it. The precise shape does not matter."

"Very well."

"Which of your two buckets weighs more, the one with the wood, or the one without?"

What do you think?

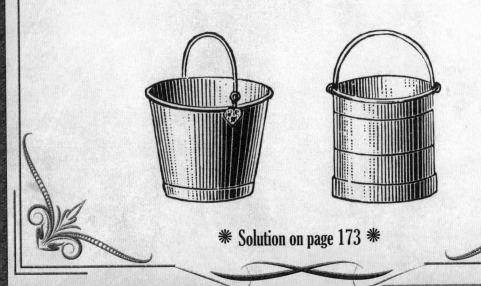

✳ Solution on page 173 ✳

THE MADDENED MILLER

One of the odder features of *The Adventure of the Wandering Bishops* was a peculiarly enraged Hookland miller. The source of his ire was, we eventually discovered, an altercation between his wife and her sister, which disrupted certain plans he had regarding the purchase of a large quantity of land. But that really is by the by.

Holmes, still in his farmer's disguise, had approached the miller with several sacks of grain, purchased earlier in return for a dozen chickens. The miller's usual tariff was one tenth part of the flour he produced for any given customer. Holmes, of course, was only too happy to pay this trifling price.

When the work was done, we found ourselves in possession of a bushel of freshly ground flour. The less said about that, the better. But my question is this. How much flour did the enraged miller claim?

✻ Solution on page 173 ✻

THE FIRST CAMOUFLAGE

I remember the day clearly, even now. It was late October, a Friday. We had finished luncheon a short while before, and I was sitting in a pleasant state of post-prandial sleepiness. I was on the verge of nodding off when Holmes loudly called out, "I've got four words for you, Watson."

I think I managed some groan of mild protest, which Holmes duly ignored.

"Elephantine. Beechwood. Bugleweed. Stepmother."

"And?" I asked.

"Each word contains a smaller word, well camouflaged within its parent. What is the common theme uniting the four smaller words?"

It was definitely not the way that I'd fondly imagined my afternoon progressing. Can you find the solution?

❊ Solution on page 173 ❊

FABULOUS

"Hubris, Watson, is one of the very heights of folly. To become so swollen with arrogance that one assumes oneself infallible – and to act or, more pertinently, fail to act as a result of that arrogance – why, that is the cause of inevitable disaster."

"Is that so?" I asked, somewhat confused.

Holmes waved a newspaper at me. "Some buffoon of a runner was so overconfident about his opponent that he opened himself to utter ridicule. According to this piece, our fellow gave his inferior rival a head-start equal to one-eighth of the length of the course. Now, they started at opposite ends for some reason, and after his late start, the superior runner ambled along with colossal contempt for his opponent. He got a nasty shock when, at just one-sixth of the way along the course, he met his rival coming the other way. He lost, of course." Holmes paused, and a glint appeared in his eye.

"Quite so," I said swiftly.

"Maybe you can tell me, old chap, how many times the buffoon would have had to increase his speed in order to win the race? Round to the nearest whole number, and let's assume that the slower man maintains the same speed throughout."

What do you think?

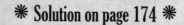

✳ **Solution on page 174** ✳

OUT EAST

Whilst doing some research during *The Nasty Affair of the Highwayman's Daughter*, I stumbled across an interesting little snippet of fact about her father's home country. It was a small, mountainous state in eastern Europe of no great political or cultural distinction, with a reputation for sullen bloodthirstiness amongst its menfolk. No great surprise, given the context in which I was examining it.

Be that as it may, the discovery I made was that in the preceding year, some 1.4 per cent of the country's women as compared to 2.1 per cent of the men had married spouses of the same nationality.

I announced this to Holmes, who immediately challenged me to deduce the comparative percentage of women in that place.

What do you think?

✳ Solution on page 174 ✳

THE SUICIDE

Inspector Lestrade of Scotland Yard was a small, lean man with a strong hint of ferret in his ancestry. Whilst his approach to crime was wholly pedestrian, he was nevertheless a tireless servant of the law. Holmes and I worked with him a number of times to bring villains to justice. Despite having received ample evidence of Holmes's brilliance however, he somehow maintained an intrinsic faith in his own opinion when it differed. So I was utterly unsurprised, during *The Adventure of the Impossible Gecko*, when he dismissed Holmes's first analysis out of hand.

"Look, Holmes, I understand that your client fears foul play. But it's a suicide, clear and simple. There's nothing here to suggest otherwise." Lestrade gestured around the study we were in. "The only thing we've moved is the deceased."

It was a dim little room, lined with book-filled cases and dominated by a leather-topped oak desk and the chair that went with it. In the centre of the desk sat a pill bottle, completely empty. The remaining couple of pills lay next to it, big white oblong things about the same size as the tip of my little finger. The rest of the bottle – twenty pills or more – had gone into our client's uncle the night before. The only other thing in the room was a sheet of financial projections, which appeared utterly dire.

"My point precisely," Holmes said, with a hint of asperity. "Surely even you, Inspector, can see that suicide is highly unlikely at the very least."

He was right, of course. Can you see what he'd spotted?

❋ Solution on page 175 ❋

SCARVES

One blustery autumn afternoon, Holmes and I were walking along the Marylebone road, past Madame Tussaud's museum of wax figures. I was struggling somewhat to keep my hat in place when a particularly savage gust whipped it straight off my head. As I stooped to retrieve it, I noticed that a lady in front of us had likewise lost her scarf, which went tumbling away down the pavement.

Holmes had noticed the errant scarf as well, and turned to me with a calculating look. "Indulge me a moment, Watson, and picture that the street was significantly more crowded, and that there were a dozen ladies who found themselves suddenly without their scarves. For that matter, let's also imagine that young Wiggins was nearby, had gathered up all the scarves, and was handing them back at random to the ladies, in hope of a penny or two for his speedy service."

Wiggins was the spokesman and putative leader of the Baker Street Irregulars, a gaggle of urchins that Holmes often recruited when in need of extra eyes or hands.

"It doesn't seem impossible," I allowed, although knowing the lad, I very much doubted he'd be quite so careless as to return the scarves randomly.

"Well, then," Holmes said, "can you calculate the probability of just eleven of the ladies receiving their correct scarves?"

To my mild surprise, I realized that I could. Can you?

✷ Solution on page 175 ✷

JOE

"I asked my nephew Joseph how old he was last Saturday," Mrs Hudson declared, having brought up some hot tea one afternoon. "You'll never believe what he told me, Doctor Watson."

———— ◆ ————

"I'm sure I shall," I reassured her. "I trust you implicitly, my dear lady."

She gave me a queer look, before continuing. "He told me, bold as brass, that three years ago he'd been seven times as old as his sister Ruthie. Then he added that two years ago, he'd been four times her age, and one year ago, just three times her age. After that outburst, he sat back and beamed at me. Well, I'm sure you'll have no trouble figuring out their ages, a learned man like yourself, but it wasn't what I was expecting, not at all." She beamed at me in turn.

Fortunately, long association with Sherlock Holmes had hardened me to this sort of challenge, and I was able to respond. Can you calculate the answer?

❋ Solution on page 175 ❋

THE WENNS

Holmes and I were lurking outside a small hotel named The Wenns in the quiet fenland town of King's Lynn. It was perhaps one of the less diverting ways of spending a Monday evening, but we were hot on the heels of the frightened carpenter's brother-in-law, whom Holmes needed to observe in the wild, as it were. The little marketplace was quaint enough, to be sure, but as the evening dragged on, I confess I was becoming rather bored.

Catching my mood, Holmes decided to give my mind something to chew on, by way of a distraction from the drizzle. "You'll have observed that the bar in there is quite crowded, Watson."

"Quite so," I replied. "Warm and dry too, no doubt."

"Indubitably. Still, let us pretend that each of the patrons has a different number of penny coins in his possession, and that there are more patrons by number than any single one of them has pennies."

There was a pause whilst I untangled this, and then I nodded.

"Now, if I tell you that none of the patrons possesses exactly 33 pennies, can you tell me how many patrons there are at most?"

"I'm sure I can, in theory at least," I replied.

"Then please do so," he said.

What is the correct answer?

✸ Solution on page 176 ✸

MAIDA VALE

During *The Adventure of the Maida Vale Baker*, Holmes tasked Wiggins and the Irregulars with observing both the baker, Gerry by name, and his dissolute cousin, James. Caution was strictly advised, as both men were prone to a certain lamentable rashness.

When Wiggins returned to 221b, he reported that Gerry had left the bakery at 9am sharp, and set off up Watling Street at a leisurely two miles an hour. An hour later, James had followed in his cousin's footsteps, but walking more briskly, at four miles an hour, and with a lovely Irish setter in tow.

The dog had immediately dashed off after the baker, and according to Wiggins's intelligence, had no sooner caught up to Gerry than it turned around and ran back to James. It then proceeded to continue running back and forth between the men – at an even ten miles per hour – until James had caught up with Gerry, at which point all three stopped entirely.

We made sense of it all in the end, but how far did the dog run?

❋ Solution on page 176 ❋

SHEEP

The thorny particulars of the inheritability of sheep became a pressing concern for Holmes and myself during the frankly rather peculiar *Adventure of the Raven Child*, which unfolded largely in the mountains of Gwynedd. A landowner with a heroic combined flock of sheep had died in bizarre circumstances after spending a night alone at the top of Cader Idris – a feat said by the locals to turn you into either a poet or a madman. As if there were a difference.

Anyhow, for the purposes of this volume, I shall spare you the convoluted details, and instead focus on the practical issue of sheep herds. The landowner's sons, David, Idris, and Caradog, all inherited a portion of their father's herd, along with the lands and tenant shepherds required to support the sheep. David, as the eldest, received twenty percent more sheep than Idris, and twenty five per cent more sheep than Caradog, the youngest brother.

If I tell you that Idris received precisely one thousand sheep, can you tell me how many Caradog inherited?

✷ Solution on page 176 ✷

THE SECOND WORDKNOT

If I recall correctly – and I am reasonably sure that I do – I was engaged in the precarious business of attempting to butter a very hot crumpet when Holmes presented me with my second wordknot. It was some weeks since I'd wrestled with the first of its kind, but the simple principle of untangling three loosely associated ten-letter words was still reasonably fresh.

"You recall, I assume, that the first letter of each word is on the first line, the second letter of each on the second line, and so on?"

I assured Holmes that I so recalled, and with that he left me to it.

1. ART
2. HOQ
3. UOU
4. RAD
5. MOM
6. AAL
7. LIR
8. TII
9. NEN
10. EES

Can you untangle the knot?

✹ Solution on page 176 ✹

THE PARTNER

Much of the nastiness surrounding *The Adventure of the Maida Vale Baker* was rooted in his business affairs. It is often the case, I have found, that the trust one places in family and friends is misplaced when it comes to affairs of the wallet. The baker, Gerry, and his cousin James had been partners in the bakery since the beginning. James provided the capital, whilst Gerry did the work and ran the business. Once the basic investment capital had been repaid, they settled on an agreement whereby Gerry owned one and a half times as much of the business as James did.

Matters did not start to get complicated until a new arrival appeared on the scene. Mr Andreas was a contact of James, a friend of a friend. A gentleman of Greek extraction, he was possessed of a certain presence that warned the discerning onlooker not to trifle with him. Sadly, neither James nor Gerry apparently had sufficient discernment.

The deal they struck was that Mr Andreas would pay the handsome sum of £1,000, and each of the three partners would then hold a one-third stake in the business. Matters quickly became unseemly.

What would have been the most equitable distribution of the money, £1,000?

✻ Solution on page 177 ✻

FRUITY

On occasion, Mrs Hudson enjoyed presenting Holmes with some small test of ingenuity, if for no other satisfaction than to take a perverse pride in how rapidly he was able to respond. Sometimes, Holmes would pass the onus of response to me, either because he deemed the matter beneath his weighty appraisal, or because of his ongoing attempts to improve my logical processes. Mrs Hudson seemed scarcely less pleased on those occasions. I assume that whatever she lost by way of Holmes's rapier mind, she made up for by watching me fumble around trying to best her.

One morning, before I'd even been able to take a cup of tea, one such conundrum winged its way towards me. I pulled myself together, looked up from my cup, and said, "I'm sorry, Mrs Hudson, could you repeat that?"

"Of course, Doctor," she replied. "I was weighing the fruit earlier, for a crumble, and it hit me. One apple and six plums were the same weight as my one pear, while all three apples and the pear were the same weight as ten plums. So I was wondering, how many plums do you think would match the weight of the pear?"

"Thank you," I said, and took a long, slow drink of tea.

What do you think the answer is?

✳ Solution on page 177 ✳

HANDS

We were introduced to an inordinately large number of people during *The Adventure of the Frightened Carpenter*. At one point, it was starting to feel as if I was going to have to personally shake hands with everybody in London. Given that several of them had insisted on attempting to crush my hand to pulp as part of the process, I was rapidly tiring of the whole affair, and made some throwaway remark to Holmes to that effect.

"Don't disparage the humble handshake, Watson," Holmes told me. "It's a vital part of the social glue that holds the city together, no matter how tiresome it might prove on occasion. Consider yourself grateful that we are not in a culture where a crushing grip is the standard of politesse."

"Oh, I am," I assured him.

"Here's a little something to take your mind off your manual weariness. Do you imagine that there are an odd or even number of people who have themselves shaken hands with an odd number of people?"

Can you deduce an answer?

✳ Solution on page 177 ✳

CIDER

Whilst in Hookland on *The Adventure of the Wandering Bishops*, Holmes made the mistake of impressing a voluble cider manufacturer with his insight. The fellow then commenced to ply us both with questions ranging from blatantly simple to utterly baffling. Most seemed to have at least some practical application. Holmes was in disguise at the time, and was forced to grit his teeth and indulge the persistent — and tipsy — fellow to avoid causing a scene. Finally he moved on, but not before both of us had comprehensively run out of patience.

One of his questions has stayed with me, perhaps because it was at least comprehensible. In the course of planting a new, square orchard with evenly spaced young trees, the fellow discovered that he had 146 trees left over unplanted. He needed to obtain a further 31 trees in order to plant them all and still have a square orchard.

How many trees had he already planted?

❋ Solution on page 178 ❋

A SENSE OF URGENCY

Holmes inevitably seized a moment when I was at my most distracted before springing his little tests and puzzles upon me. I asked him about this once, and his reply was something to the effect that observation and deduction were frequently required at times when the pressure was greatest. By interrupting me when my mind was elsewhere, he hoped to strengthen my logical faculties to work under duress. I could see the sense in it, but it was often damnably inconvenient.

I was in the middle of making notes upon an intriguing yet highly convoluted article in *The Lancet* when Holmes dashed over with a scrap of paper and thrust it under my nose. He even made his voice sound concerned. "Quick, Watson! Hurry! What's the answer?"

The paper bore this inscription:

10*9*8*7*6*5*4*3*2*1*0*–1*–2=X

What's X?

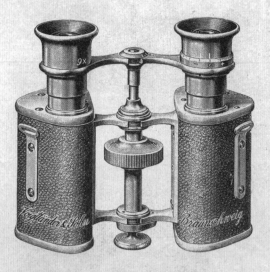

❋ Solution on page 178 ❋

HOT AND COLD

Sherlock and I were taking tea one chilly January morning when he looked up from studying his cup, to turn his attention to the frosty window. "We place a kettle or a pot on top of the hob in order to heat up. In earlier times, people hung their cauldrons and kettles over fireplaces. Not right in the middle of them, but over them."

"Quite so," I agreed. "More convenient or more effective. Or both."

"Both," he agreed. "But imagine for a moment that you have a cube of metal, say, that you wish to cool, and a block of ice that you have to keep intact. How would you arrange the two for greatest efficiency?"

"Well, I'd..." I trailed off, to think about the matter.

What is the best option?

✳ Solution on page 178 ✳

ON THE BUSES

During *The Affair of the Frightened Carpenter*, Holmes had cause to invest some time into studying the movements of a fellow named Sam Smith. It left Holmes somewhat waspish, because it transpired that Smith was in the frugal habit of travelling by bus to his appointments, and walking back from them on foot.

———◆◆◆———

On the second day, the combined travel time was precisely eight hours. Holmes also had to spend 90 minutes loitering outside a lumber merchant's depot, but that's by the by. Given that the bus managed an average of 9 mph, and Smith's walking rate was a third of that, how far did Holmes have to walk while trailing the man?

❋ Solution on page 178 ❋

HOOKLAND KNIGHTS

A lead followed during *The Adventure of the Wandering Bishops* brought us to a rather unusual under-chapel below the streets of Weychester. Three sarcophagi carved to look like armoured crusader knights dominated a small room off the main chapel.

Beneath the feet of each knight was a set of finely carved numbers. On the first was the group 30, 68, 89. On the second, the numbers 18, 23, 42. The third bore the numbers 11, 41, 74.

At the end of the small room, the wall held a dozen carved stone heads in a straight line across its middle. Each of the heads was clearly modelled after a different individual. Every face bore an expression of unsettling glee, however. It was most unpleasant. Above the heads was painted the number 16, in white, a good foot high.

"Clearly, a reference to..." Holmes stopped mid-sentence. "Watson, this should exercise you. Which knight is that painted number pointing us to?"

✳ Solution on page 179 ✳

THE THIRD WORDKNOT

Holmes's third wordknot came to me as we sat down to suffer through a thoroughly uninspired performance of an already lacklustre operetta. Normally you would never have found either of us within 50 feet of such a performance, but Holmes was on the trail of a decrepit raven-seller, and, well, there we were. I was actually glad of the distraction his puzzle afforded me, even though the unfortunate wailings made it difficult to concentrate.

The letters from which I had to disentangle three related ten-letter words, one letter each per line, were:

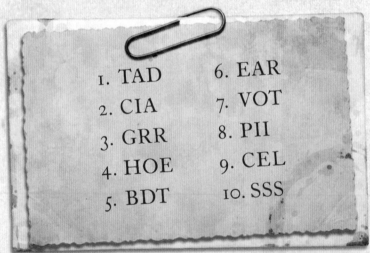

1. TAD
2. CIA
3. GRR
4. HOE
5. BDT

6. EAR
7. VOT
8. PII
9. CEL
10. SSS

Can you work out what the words were?

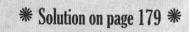

✳ Solution on page 179 ✳

THE PAINTING

A fellow came to me once looking to sell a rather handsome portrait that had been in his family for some time. This was nothing to do with a case of Holmes'. He was a patient of mine at my practice, and had noticed that I had a selection of artworks adorning the walls of my office and treatment room.

———————

Whilst the picture was undeniably attractive, his asking price was not – £640. Well, half a year's income is a ludicrous amount of money for a piece of art, so of course I declined pleasantly. Two weeks later he was back, and had dropped his asking price to a "mere" £400. Once again, I conveyed my regrets. After two more weeks, he returned, utterly unabashed, and offered me the piece for £250. On his second visit after that, I finally gave in and purchased the piece.

To the nearest whole pound, how much did I pay?

✳ Solution on page 179 ✳

DANIEL

I was reading the newspaper one afternoon when a rather grizzly little news story caught my eye. It concerned the unfortunate fate of one Daniel Boutros, the son of a rather wealthy shipping broker.

Young Mr Boutros had been to Essex on a climbing trip with a companion. Despite being generally considered skilled at the sport, something had gone wrong, and he had fallen from the top of an escarpment. His friend Alan Dickey, the lead climber, had already reached the top and was belaying Boutros from up there when the rope failed.

This was, of course, very sad, but what startled me were the florid lengths to which the newspaper reporter went in describing the scene. Several paragraphs were devoted in their entirety to poor Boutros's body, and the way it lay shattered over the mounds of coiled rope at the foot of the cliff. The friend, Dickey, was said to be in shock.

I mentioned the piece to Holmes, who grunted noncommittally. After a moment, he asked if there was any mention of a frayed rope-end. I scanned through, and sure enough, the reporter did mention frayed pieces of unwound rope.

"It's still murder," Holmes said.

Can you see why he came to that conclusion?

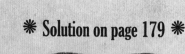 ❋ Solution on page 179 ❋

STRAIGHTFORWARD
PUZZLES

THE PLEASANT LAKE

The Peculiar Case of the Raven Child dragged Holmes and myself up to the Gwynedd village of Abergynolwyn. A devilishly long way to go, but Holmes insisted we had to see some details for ourselves. So one grey morning, we found ourselves in a small chapel on the shores of a glacial lake, the Tal-y-Llyn, where the River Dysynni begins.

Inside the chapel, a simple altar bore an exhortation regarding the ten commandments, along with the customary cloth and Bible. Above it, on the wall, a curious message was chiselled, clearly of some age:

P R S V R Y P R F C T M N
V R K P T H S P R C P T S T

Holmes glanced at it, and his eyes narrowed for a moment. Then he turned to me, with a certain light in his eye. "That last line is missing a final 'N'," he said.

"Clearly that's not all that's missing," I replied.

"I'll grant you that," he said. "There's precisely one other letter missing too – more than a dozen copies of it."

He would say no more, and we had to sit there until I'd decoded the message. It was not a comfortable time. Can you tell what the message is?

✳ Solution on page 182 ✳

THE UNCLE

We were walking through the cemetery at Paddington Green, looking for the headstone of a carpenter's uncle. There was some doubt as to the date of that worthy's final repose, and we had resolved to go straight to the source. As it transpired, our efforts were fruitless. Secretly, the man had been alive for years, living with another family in Hadleigh.

As we passed a rather extravagant carving of an old, bearded man in a humble robe, Holmes nodded to himself.

"Here's a simple little matter for you to chew on, Watson."

I nodded. "Very well, old chap."

"Let us posit that a particular fellow has spent a fifth of his life as a child, a quarter as a youth, a third as a man, and thirteen years in decline. How old must he be?"

Can you find the answer?

✳ Solution on page 182 ✳

SLICK

Picking my way cautiously down Baker Street in the icy February morning was always a trying experience. It didn't help much that Holmes often appeared to have the feet of a cat, and hardly ever slipped around. I, on the other hand, typically felt in serious danger of crashing to the ground with every step I took.

———————

One morning, Holmes took note of my stumbling and suggested that I attempt to walk on the slickest, smoothest patches of ice I could find, rather than preferring those patches with a little texture to offer grip.

I, in turn, suggested that I was having enough trouble as it was.

"But, my dear chap, you'll find the smooth stuff easier to walk on than the rough. The smoother, the better."

He was right, as he inevitably is. Can you say why?

THE SECOND CAMOUFLAGE

I was sorting through my pocket change, which had become annoyingly weighty, when Holmes inflicted his third set of camouflage words on me. "Heartbreaker, journeyers, solipsistic and diagnoses," he declared. Having pulled my wits together and confirmed that I was supposed to locate the four small, thematically linked words hiding within each of the longer ones, I had him repeat them to me.

———————

Can you find the answer?

❋ Solutions on page 182 ❋

FORTY-FIVE

Holmes picked a slice of toast from the breakfast rack, but instead of buttering it, he thoughtfully tore it into four uneven pieces, and tossed them onto the tray.

"Mrs Hudson won't like that, old chap," I warned him. "You know how she is about food vandalism."

"Forty-five," he replied.

I blinked.

"Curious number," he said. "Of course, they all are."

"Of course," I muttered, under my breath.

"You can split 45 into four chunks, four different natural numbers that added together produce it as their total. So far, so true of anything over 9. But these particular four numbers are somewhat special. Add 2 to the first, subtract 2 from the second, the third multiply by 2, and the fourth divide by 2. The result of each four operations is the same. Can you tell me the numbers?"

"I dare say," I replied. "May I finish my egg first?"

"If you must."

What are the four numbers in question?

✳ Solution on page 183 ✳

ST MARY AXE

Holmes was reading a file that Inspector Lestrade had furnished him with some high-profile matter regarding purloined diaries belonging to a cabinet minister's younger daughter. Every so often, he'd snort or toss his head, rather like an ill-tempered stallion. Finally, he put the papers down, and turned to me. "Lestrade's documents say that Mr Lloyd takes precisely four hours to walk to and from his home in Stoke Newington to the City, not counting the 60 seconds he takes to hand an envelope to a small man in St Mary Axe. His outward journey is conducted at an average rate of five miles per hour, and the return journey three."

———◆———

"Is that useful to know?" I asked innocently.

"Not in the least," Holmes replied. "Maybe you'd tell me how far it is from Lloyd's home to his small man in the city?"

Can you find the answer?

❋ Solution on page 183 ❋

GREAT-AUNT ADA

Mrs Hudson's steely gaze flicked to the mangled toast on the tray, and her eyes narrowed. "Have I ever told you gentlemen about my Great-Aunt Ada?" she asked, voice deceptively mild.

———◆———

I winced, and shook my head. "I don't believe so, Mrs Hudson."

"She's 45 years older than I am. Always has been, of course. But she's getting a little long in the tooth, and this year, if you take her age and swap the digits, you end up with my age. Curious." She paused for a moment. "Both the digits are primes, too," she added primly.

Holmes just snorted, leaving me to work out her Great-Aunt Ada's age. Can you do it?

✳ Solution on page 183 ✳

RONNIE

Mrs Hudson was in high dudgeon over the supposedly high-handed way that one of her cousins, a gardener out in the Home Counties, had been treated by his latest employer.

———◆◆———

"Ronnie agreed an annual salary of £500 plus a rather nice all-weather cape with the Terringtons. In the end, he had to leave them after seven months, because my uncle Hob had a nasty turn. The Terringtons gave him just £60, on top of the cape. Sixty quid! That's less than ten pounds a month. It's a disgrace."

"That's dreadful," I sympathized, but I'll admit that at the same time, I was wondering precisely how expensive the cape actually was.

Assuming the Terringtons are playing fair, what's the cape worth?

FEBRUARY

I was reading *The Times* of London when Holmes, having glanced at the date on the front of the paper, said, "Did you know that the last time we had a February with five Wednesdays in it was in 1888?"

———◆◆———

Having given myself a moment to process this information, I confirmed that no, in fact I had not been consciously aware of that fact.

"It may interest you to calculate when the next occasion will be," Holmes continued.

Whilst I did not feel that the matter was especially fascinating, I went ahead and worked it out. Can you?

❋ Solutions on page 184 ❋

ISAAC

"Catch!" Holmes tossed an apple in my general direction.

I caught it shortly before it struck me in the chest.

He nodded. "You know, I trust, that everything falls at the same speed."

"Well, I seem to remember hearing something of the sort," I replied. "But drop a tumbler of scotch and a piece of paper, and tell me that again."

Holmes smiled. "Experimentation. Good. I should say then, that apart from the effects of air resistance, everything falls at the same speed. Gravity pulls on every atom of an object simultaneously, not just the ones on the outer surface."

"Hmm," I said. "Well, if you say so. It seems a little counter-intuitive, however."

"Indeed it does, Watson. Indeed it does. So, experimentation. Can you devise an experiment we can perform here and now?"

❈ Solution on page 184 ❈

THE CODE

We came across an encrypted sales ledger whilst investigating *The Adventure of the Frightened Carpenter*. It wasn't especially challenging to decode, but it was interesting, so I shall present a sample to you here for your amusement and possible edification:

$$GAUNT +$$
$$OILER =$$
$$\overline{RGUOEI}$$

The trick to the code was reasonably straightforward. The fellow had selected a common ten-letter English word, one in which all the letters were different, and then assigned the digits from 1 up to 9 and then 0 to the letters. He then simply substituted the appropriate letter for each digit.

On that basis, can you find the key word?

✳ Solution on page 185 ✳

THE TRACK

Our pursuit of the dubious Alan Grey, whom we encountered during *The Adventure of the Third Carriage*, led Holmes and myself to a circular running track where, as the sun fell, we witnessed a race using bicycles. There was some sort of substantial wager involved in the matter, as I recall, and the track had been closed off specially for the occasion. This was insufficient to prevent our ingress, obviously.

One of the competitors was wearing red, and the other blue. We never did discover their names. As the race started, red immediately pulled ahead. A few moments later, Holmes observed that if they maintained their pace, red would complete a lap in four minutes, whilst blue would complete one in seven.

Having made that pronouncement, he turned to me. "How long would it be before red passed blue if they kept those rates up, old chap?"

Whilst I wrestled with the answer, Holmes went back to watching the proceedings.

Can you find the solution?

✳ Solution on page 185 ✳

A CHELSEA TALE

"My Angie's fella, Trevor," said Mrs Hudson, "He's got a pal named Rick, and it was Rick's sister Sally who told me about the brother of her cousin's best friend, Roderick."

"Um, is that the cousin, the best friend, or the brother?" I asked, starting to sink.

Mrs Hudson gave me a very pitying look. "Roddie? He's Budgie's friend. Lovely lad, he is, specially considering."

I thought about asking what I was supposed to consider, but decided discretion in this instance was the better part of valour.

"Anyhow," she continued. "Roddie knows this guy who works out in Chelsea, if you can believe it."

That seemed entirely plausible, and I nodded accordingly.

"Well, Sally was telling me that Jez – that's the Chelsea chap, Doctor – got such a nasty fright at work the other day from a gigantic hornet the size of a robin that he leapt straight through the window he was standing at. It's eight floors up, Doctor."

"That's terrible," I said, genuinely shocked. "Poor man."

"Yes. He was sacked straight away, of course."

"Wait," I said, swinging back to total confusion. "What? Sacked? Wasn't he killed?"

"Killed? Not hardly. He a small cut on his ear from the glass, but no, otherwise he was totally fine."

"I don't understand," I had to confess. Do you?

✳ **Solution on page 186** ✳

EXPRESS

Holmes and I were on the Waterloo train, out of Westchester. It was a slow service for a non-stopping express, managing a speed of precisely 40 miles per hour, or so Holmes assured me anyway. We'd been travelling for a little over an hour when a train in the opposite direction thundered past, heading into Hookland. That one, he informed me, was the faster express, travelling at 60 miles an hour, having left Waterloo more than two hours before.

By this point, I was anticipating a test of my reasoning, possibly algebraic in nature, and Holmes didn't disappoint.

"How far apart were the two trains an hour ago, Watson?"

Can you find the answer?

✳ Solution on page 186 ✳

THE FENCE

Wiggins, the chief scamp of the Baker Street Irregulars, was reporting to us regarding movements afoot in Highgate cemetery. He looked unusually weary, but no less alert or mischievous for that.

"They're putting up some sort of statue, Mr Holmes," the boy said.

"I knew it," Holmes replied. "Are they fencing it off?"

"They are, sir. But they're having trouble."

Holmes perked up. "Oh? How so?"

"Well, they clearly want to use all the posts they have, and make an even fence. I heard one of 'em moaning that at a foot apart, they had 150 posts too few, whilst at a yard, they had 70 too many."

Our discussion went on for some time, but let me ask you this – how many posts did the would-be fencers have?

THE FOURTH WORDKNOT

Holmes and I were in a comfortable tea-house with a clear line of sight to the front doors of St Paul's Cathedral. *The Adventure of the Impossible Gecko* had taken an unexpectedly clerical turn, and some extended observation was in order. When Holmes handed me a slip of paper, I at first mistakenly assumed it was something to do with the matter at hand. Not so. It was the fourth wordknot.

"You know the drill, Watson. Three loosely linked ten-letter words, first letters jumbled on the first row, you have to unpick them."

"Quite," I said, taking the paper. It read:

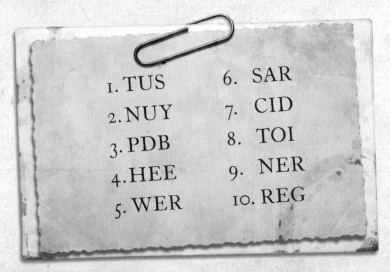

1. TUS
2. NUY
3. PDB
4. HEE
5. WER
6. SAR
7. CID
8. TOI
9. NER
10. REG

Can you find the solution?

✳ Solution on page 187 ✳

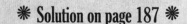

THE ONE

"Many numbers have plausible claims to interest," Holmes told me.

---◆◆◆---

I nodded, passingly familiar with some of the eccentricities of the mathematician's art.

"This one, however, is quite unique. Can you perhaps tell me why?"

He handed me a notepad, on which he had written the number 8,549,176,320.

Do you know what he was getting at?

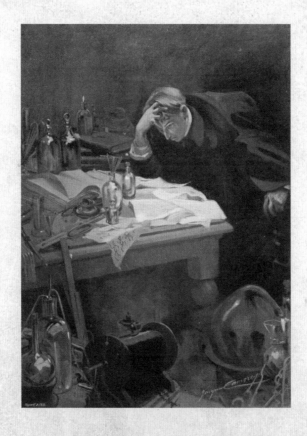

✳ Solution on page 187 ✳

THE BISCUITS

Wiggins told us about an altercation amongst the Irregulars which had fallen to him to mediate. A small sack of biscuits had gone missing from their collective supplies, and it could have been any one of six suspects.

When he discussed the matter with the six, their stories boiled down to the following six statements:

Will: Stephen did it.

Max: Robin did it.

Mary: Will did it.

Stephen: I didn't do it.

Gwen: Max did it.

Robin: Yeah, Max did it.

His main annoyance with the affair was that only one of the six told him the truth. He immediately discerned the guilty party from that, of course. Can you?

✻ Solution on page 187 ✻

DANGEROUS LADIES

Holmes watched Mrs Hudson depart from our rooms with a somewhat rueful expression. "On the subject of redoubtable women, Watson, I have a little mental exercise for you. Two of the most formidable women in ancient history were undoubtedly Cleopatra, the last pharaoh of Egypt, and our very own Boadicea, who razed Colchester, London and St Albans to the ground."

"My word," I said. "There's a lesson there, Holmes – don't mess with a Norfolk lass."

He shot me a dark look before continuing. "Our best estimates say that the two ladies had a combined lifespan of 69 years. We know that Cleopatra died in 30 BC, and that Boadicea's death came 129 years after Cleopatra's birth. So when was Boadicea born?"

Can you find the answer?

❋ Solution on page 187 ❋

SQUARE SHEEP

"Intuition," Holmes told me, "is just a way of saying that your brain spotted an answer that your conscious mind did not. It can be a powerful aid to deduction for those in whom the awareness is less than perfectly honed, provided that you are ever-vigilant for the differences between a genuine intuition and simple imagination. Telling the two apart is a matter of practice."

———— ◆◆◆ ————

So saying, he tossed me a box of matches. "Thanks," I said, somewhat doubtfully.

"Four of those, Watson, will make you a square. If you fancy a practical application, imagine that they are fences, and you are marking off a pen for a sheep or goat. Better yet, let us say that each match is the equivalent of a yard in length, in which case our square is one square yard in area."

"Square sheep, perhaps?" I offered.

"Say rather enormously fat sheep. Your challenge is to discover the minimum number of matches required to make a closed shape of at least ten square yards in area – a pen for ten of your obese sheep. You are not allowed to break the matches, by the by."

It took me a lot of trial and error before Holmes was satisfied with my efforts. Can you find a solution?

✳ Solution on page 188 ✳

MR ANDREAS

During *The Adventure of the Maida Vale Baker*, we had to look into the financial affairs of Mr Andreas. They proved quite surprisingly regular, in the mathematical sense of the word. Some fifteen years before, the man had started an investment firm with his capital, of £1,600. His wealth then proceeded to grow by exactly 55 per cent every three years. It was quite uncanny how precise this was.

There was a reason for that, of course.

But for now, can you say to the nearest pound how much money Mr Andreas had after fifteen years?

❋ Solution on page 188 ❋

THE BOTTLE

Holmes said something quiet, and I looked up to see a bottle arcing through the air towards me. Luckily I had my hands free, so I managed to catch it, rather than just being clunked in the chest. It was clear glass, with a flat, circular base and straight sides which led up to a complicated, twisty neck, and a stoppered opening. It was about one-third full of water, or something that looked like water anyway.

———— ◆·◆·◆ ————

"Well caught, Watson", said Holmes in a more normal volume. I frowned at him.

"I see that there is a ruler beside you," he continued. "Without opening the bottle or immersing it in any way, can you tell me the volume of liquid that it would hold when full?"

I was able to do so. Would you have been so able?

❋ Solution on page 189 ❋

DAVEY

Wiggins had finished describing his latest discoveries to us, and rather than take off, he hung around to share an anecdote. "A funny thing happened to me on the south bank this morning, Mr Holmes."

"Is that so?"

"On my honour," Wiggins said, with an impish grin. "I was almost up to opposite the palace of Westminster when I happened to glance over my shoulder, and saw my old pal Davey heading in my direction, about 200 yards away. So I turned around, and headed towards him. Two hundred yards of facing each other later, him grinning at me every step we took, he was still 200 yards away. Can you credit it?"

"Very rum," Holmes said, allowing himself a small smile.

He had to explain it to me, but can you see what had happened?

✳ Solution on page 189 ✳

THE WATCH

The Adventure of the Frightened Carpenter led Holmes and myself to a warehouse, as I may have mentioned before. One of the more interesting things about that operation was the somewhat convoluted schedule that the four watchmen had devised for themselves. Their employers required that each man work two six-hour shifts a day with a break in between, starting precisely on the hour, so that there were always two men on duty, and both never changed shift at the same time.

As we discovered later, each of the four men had their own personal requirements regarding their working hours. Jim wanted to start at midnight, and be entirely done by 4 p.m.; Dave wanted to be free between 10 a.m. and 4 p.m.; Peter wanted to relieve Dave after his second shift; Mike, finally, had to be on duty at 9 a.m..

What shift pattern did they finally settle on?

✳ Solution on page 189 ✳

THE FIFTH WORDKNOT

I received my fifth wordknot from Holmes over a rather nice luncheon at the Great Western Hotel at Paddington, a rather fine example of mid-century Second Empire architecture and design, with lavish ornamentation. The hotel, that is, rather than the luncheon, which was nevertheless quite outstanding.

I did my best to address Holmes's challenge adroitly, but I must confess that the goose was quite a distraction. The note he gave me is replicated below, and the task, as I'm sure you recall, is to unpick the three ten-letter words whose letters are scrambled in the ten rows below, first letters on the first row, second letters on the second row, and so on. The words are of course thematically related.

1. CTV
2. WHO
3. LAI
4. TUT
5. BTT
6. IEI
7. LRN
8. IEI
9. STN
10. GYS

✻ Solution on page 189 ✻

THE LEASE

Mrs Hudson was cleaning away our breakfast things. "That Archie, he does think he's a wit. Well, he's half-right."

"Archie?" I asked, in a moment of incaution.

"A cousin, on Mr Hudson's side," she said.

I breathed a sigh of relief. "How many cousins do you actually have, Mrs Hudson?" I couldn't help myself.

"Seventy-nine," she told me. "No, make that 78. That fool Neill died last month. Fell off a cliff. There's only 22 as I'd consider top shelf, though. Anyway, I was telling you about Archie."

"Indeed you were," I admitted.

"Well, Archie lives in a small place up Wembley way. He's on a 99-year lease, and I thought to ask him how much time there was left on it. So he only tells me, all smug like, that two-thirds of the time that's expired is equal to four-fifths of the time remaining. Of course, a gentleman like yourself wouldn't be fazed by that for an instant, would you?"

"Of course not," I managed. Holmes snickered from across the room.

How long is left on the lease?

※ **Solution on page 190** ※

TEA

Holmes turned to look at me, fixing me with his gaze until I lowered my book. "Have you ever considered the plight of the humble grocer, Watson?"

I admitted that I had not, in general, spent a great deal of time attempting to evaluate the life of grocers, no.

"Scales can be a positively devilish business," he said.

"Is that so?"

"Most definitely. Imagine that you are such a grocer, in urgent need of dividing a twenty-pound bale of tea into two-pound packets. The only weights you have to use on your scale are one weighing nine pounds, and one weighing five pounds. What would be the least number of weighings you would need to divide up your bale correctly?"

What do you think?

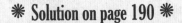

✳ Solution on page 190 ✳

LOOSE CHANGE

It occurs to me that an experience of my own may prove a worthy addition to this collection of problems. When I returned home to 221b from the trip to Hookland, I found myself rather short on ready money. I had kept receipts and other notes, so I had a solid idea of where it had all gone.

At the start of the journey, my ticket from Hookland back to London cost me precisely one half of the money I had available. Before boarding, I also bought a fortifying mug of tea for Holmes and myself, at a cost of sixpence. When we arrived back in London, it was lunchtime, so I treated the pair of us to a pub lunch at Waterloo, which cost me half of what I had remaining, plus ten further pence to boot. Half of what that left me went on getting back across town to Paddington. Then I gave sixpence to an old beggar outside the station, and paid nine pence for a quick shoe-shine. When I got home, I discovered that I had just one solitary sixpence left.

How much did I start out with? Feel free to calculate the sum in pennies.

✳ Solution on page 190 ✳

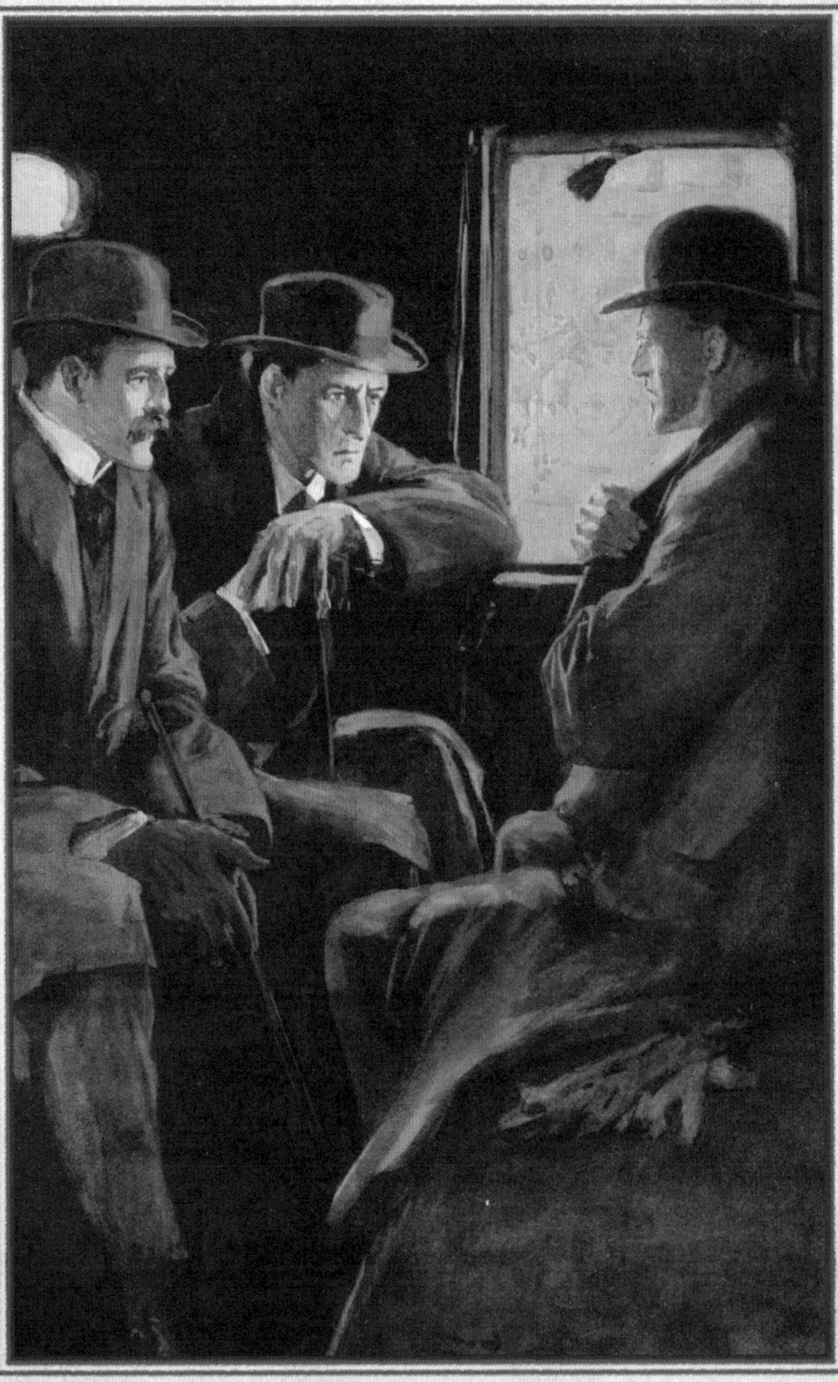

HOW MANY COWS

During *The Adventure of the Wandering Bishops*, Holmes disguised himself as a Hookland farmer, and demonstrated an astonishing mastery of the frankly baffling local dialect. On those occasions where he had conversations with his supposed peers – as happened with alarming regularity – I was frequently left at a complete loss as to the topic of discussion. Still, our subterfuge proved a very useful necessity in coming to grips with the elusive self-professed major, C. L. Nolan, and his trail of intrigue and terror. But I must not permit myself to get distracted.

After one encounter with a fellow with the unlikely name of Podge, Holmes confessed that they'd been discussing theoretical cows.

"Mr Podge seemed most concerned regarding his black woodland cow," he told me. "He said that this beast had started producing one female calf a year, from the age of two, and to his apparent distress, each of these female calves had grown to follow the exact pattern of their mother, as had their own offspring, and so on. He was particularly worried about the time, 25 years from the birth of the black woodland cow, when apparently 'the time would be right', whatever that may denote."

"My word," I said. "Queer fellow. Wouldn't half of them have died of old age, or been eaten, or something?"

"He seemed to think that they would all – of some inevitability – still be alive. How many female cows would we be talking about at this point?"

Can you find the answer?

✳ Solution on page 191 ✳

ODD

Holmes was clutching some sort of disturbingly decorated thurible, and holding forth on the vital necessity of allowing one's mind to think outside of the rigidly inflexible train-tracks of conventional thought. The thurible, which had come from an abandoned church, was glittering in the sunlight as he waved it around the drawing-room. It kept drawing my eye, to my annoyance, as the peculiar script with which it was engraved made me feel more than a little uneasy.

"The superior mind must not be blinkered, Watson. Watson?"

"Ah, yes, Holmes. Not blinkered. Quite so."

"I'm glad you agree," he said, tossing the glittering censer from one hand to the other and back. "So. Write down five odd digits for me that will add up to fourteen."

I paused at that. "An odd number of odd numbers coming up even? That's impossible, surely?"

Holmes sighed. "What was I just saying?"

Can you find a solution?

✷ Solution on page 191 ✷

DRAFT

March was approaching slowly, and the weather outside was frightful. Snow, snow and more snow had been piling up for days, and despite the well-heaped fireplace, 221b was decidedly chilly. Holmes was standing by the window, gazing out onto the street, and making quiet deductions to himself about passing strangers, as was his occasional habit. Then he turned to face me.

"You'll have noticed that there's a cold draft coming from the window, my dear friend."

"I have indeed," I said.

"I can assure you that the window is perfectly sound, mechanically. There is no gap or chink in either glass or woodwork. So where's the draft coming from?"

That floored me for a bit. What do you think?

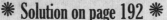

❋ Solution on page 192 ❋

THE SEAMSTRESS

During *The Adventure of the Impossible Gecko*, we interviewed a seamstress who'd seen a suspicious man loitering around outside her employers' manor house in rural Essex. The house was robbed a day later, and a priceless jewel-studded jade gecko – which really ought not to have existed, given all historical precedent – went missing. Naturally, the Turners recalled the information that the seamstress had passed to them the night before, so it was a clear necessity that we interview her.

When she arrived at 221b Baker Street, Miss Adams seemed polite and pleasant, if somewhat over-awed. Holmes looked her over, and spotted several sure signs of her profession, including needle-spotting on the second joint of her thumb, and a very specific callus on her index finger. Comfortable with her bona fides, he interviewed her.

We learnt from Miss Adams that it was a drizzly night when she saw the man out on the grounds, observing the house. She was working in a room on the ground floor, and caught sight of him near the tree-line, some 40 feet away. Although she was unable to see the man's face, she said that he was around six feet in height, and strongly built. He watched the house for several minutes, before turning around and slinking away. She immediately went to inform the Turners.

As soon as she left the building, Holmes leapt to his feet, grabbed a tattered coat from a closet, and dashed after her. All he'd spare me by way of explanation was that she was clearly lying. Can you say why?

✳ Solution on page 192 ✳

BEES

"It's interesting," Holmes said, "the lengths to which people will go in order to obfuscate perfectly simple information."

"Imagine that," I said.

"Well, Watson, you of all people should be highly familiar with such manipulations." I must have looked slightly dismayed at that, for he followed up swiftly. "Having spent so much time exposed to academic research during your medical training."

"Ah. Yes, that. Damnable stuff, Holmes. Self-aggrandizement at its worst, often."

"Precisely." Holmes nodded. "Take this, which comes from a letter I received from an apiarist I have been corresponding with in Devon. He says, of a small hive, that one-fifth of the workers typically went to his azaleas, one-third to his roses, and a number equal to three times the difference between these two fractions to his geraniums, leaving the remaining worker to dart about uncertainly."

"Does he now?" I asked. "I suppose you'd like me to tell you how many worker bees there were in total?"

"Excellent, Watson. Indeed I would."

Any idea?

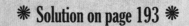
❋ **Solution on page 193** ❋

FRUITFUL

Holmes had been downstairs to have a word with Mrs Hudson regarding cabbage, and returned carrying a large orange.

———————◆◆◆———————

"Did you settle the cabbage matter to your satisfaction, old chap?" I asked him.

"Quite so," he replied. "That woman is a fountain of information."

"Indeed she is," I agreed, thinking of her frequent tales of her bewildering assortment of relatives and their in-laws.

"Did you know that she keeps a bowl of fruit downstairs?"

"Of course," I said.

"There's a number of pieces of fruit in there today. Given my depredations, all but two of them are oranges, all but two of them are pears, and all but two of them are apples. How many is that?"

Can you find the solution?

✳ Solution on page 193 ✳

THE THIRD CAMOUFLAGE

I was returning home from a shopping trip, carrying several quite sizeable bags, when Holmes accosted me on the street just outside the door to 221b. "Wait, Watson. Do not enter!"

I flinched slightly, surprised at his appearance, and stopped where I was.

"Tourbillion," barked Holmes. "Underfunded. Candyfloss. Tessellated."

After my initial panicked moment where I feared the poor fellow had suffered a major stroke, I realized that he was assigning me one of his camouflage puzzles. Four words, each containing a smaller word, such that the smaller words are thematically linked. I confess that my relief at his ongoing wellbeing quite drove the words from my mind, and it was quite a fight to retrieve them.

What was the uniting theme?

✳ Solution on page 193 ✳

SPEED

Speed was something of an issue to the Baker Street Irregulars. When one lives as a street urchin, a swift pair of heels is an extremely important quality. So the Irregulars often engaged in competitive sprints — not so much for status, but to ascertain whose skills were more suited for which types of endeavour.

On one afternoon, Wiggins told us about some of that morning's races. The fastest member of the Irregulars was a twelve-year-old named Sid, who'd somehow found his way to London from Newcastle-upon-Tyne. He'd been putting a new recruit, named Raymond, to the test. In a series of 100-yard sprints, Sid had consistently beaten Ray by ten yards. Having seen Sid run, I was duly impressed by Ray's performance.

"At the end, after their rest break, Ray wanted one fair crack," Wiggins said. "So he asked Sid to start ten yards behind the line." He and Holmes both chuckled.

"I'm sure you can see what the outcome was, old chap," Holmes said to me. I snapped off an answer, and immediately regretted it. Can you find the solution?

✳ Solution on page 193 ✳

CUNNING PUZZLES

THE WEIGHTS

Mrs Hudson paused in the doorway to our rooms. "My cousin Amy's youngest turned 3 yesterday," she declared.

"Oh, congratulations," I said. Even as I said it, it occurred to me that it was a slightly fatuous comment.

"Thank you," she replied. "To mark the occasion, Amy and her husband Ben decided to measure the youngster's weight. They managed to find a public weighing machine, but from then on, things became somewhat troublesome. The family dog, Rebel, was with them, and true to his name he refused to take the matter seriously. In the end, the best that Amy could do was to get both child and husband weighed together with the dog, for a grand total of 180 lb."

"An impressive weight for a three-year-old," I observed.

"Yes, well, I was able to ascertain from Amy that Ben and the child together outweighed Rebel by 162 lb, and that the dog weighed just 30 per cent of the child's weight."

What is the weight of the child?

✳ Solution on page 196 ✳

SOLARIS

Holmes has never been especially interested in matters astronomical. He maintains – and not without a certain justification, I suppose – that the revolutions of the heavenly bodies have very little impact on the solving of crimes. He knows the moon's phases, and is aware of upcoming eclipses, but otherwise maintains that he cares little for which astronomical body moves around which, or how swiftly.

Whilst I empathize with his focus, I feel a little differently. We live in a magnificent universe, and it seems a shame to me to not pay at least a little attention to its wonders. There is little so awe-inspiring, to my mind, as gazing up at a sky full of uncountable stars, knowing that any of them might be home to a planet with an intelligent being looking in my direction.

You know, I trust, that the Earth revolves upon its axis once per day – that being how the day is formed – as well as rotating entirely around the Sun once a year, in a counterclockwise direction. So my question is this: Does your speed of rotation (in relation to the Sun) change during the day, and if so, at what time are you moving the fastest?

✷ Solution on page 196 ✷

A WORSHIP OF WRITERS

During *The Adventure of the Third Carriage*, we found ourselves attempting to unravel the specific details of a collection of writers who came by train into London. The six of them entirely filled one compartment of the carriage, seated as there were in two rows of three, facing each other.

———— ◆ ◆ ◆ ————

The facts that we managed to glean from the ticket inspector and other passers by are these. The six men were called Tomkins, Archer, Squires, Whitely, Appleby and Gardner. Between them, their specialities covered short stories, histories, humour, novels, plays and poetry, and each was reading the latest work of one of the others in the carriage.

Squires was reading a work by the person sitting opposite him. Tomkins, who is not the historian, was reading a volume of short stories. Archer, the novelist's brother-in-law, was sitting between the humorist and the short-story writer, who, in turn, was opposite the historian. Whitely was reading a play and sitting opposite the novelist. Appleby, reading the humorous book, was next to the playwright. Tomkins was sitting in a corner. Gardner, finally, hated poetry.

Who was the novelist?

❊ Solution on page 197 ❊

LOGGERS

In Sussex, Holmes and I ran into a pair of woodcutters named Doug and Dave. There was an air of the unreliable about them – not helped by a clearly discernable aroma of scrumpy – but they nevertheless proved extremely helpful in guiding us to a particular hilltop clearing some distance outside of the town of Arundel. A shadowy group had been counterfeiting sorceries of a positively medieval kind, and all sorts of nastiness had ensued.

The Adventure of the Black Alchemist is not one that I would feel comfortable recounting, and if my life never drags me back to Chanctonbury Ring I shall be a happy man. But there is still some instructive material here. Whilst we were ascending our hill, Doug and Dave made conversation by telling us about their trade. According to these worthies, working together they were able to saw 600 cubic feet of wood into large logs over the course of a day, or split as much as 900 cubic feet of logs into chunks of firewood.

Holmes immediately suggested that they saw as much wood in the first part of the day as they would need in order to finish splitting it at the end of the day. It naturally fell to me to calculate precisely how much wood that would be.

Can you find the answer?

❋ Solution on page 197 ❋

THE SIXTH WORDKNOT

I was in a tailor's shop on Jermyn Street when Holmes sprang his sixth wordknot upon me. In fact, I was being fitted for a jacket, and the tailor was most strict that I withhold from moving. It certainly made it harder to concentrate, and not having access to a pencil didn't help one bit, I can assure you. I wasn't even able to take the slip of paper, which Holmes cheerfully held out in front of me for reference.

I impose no such unreasonable strictures upon you.

As before, the slip of paper bore ten rows of three letters, each one containing one letter, in normal sequence, of a ten-letter word. The letters in each row were in no particular order, however, making the task of unscrambling the three loosely themed words quite challenging.

The rows were as follows:

1. PTV
2. IRI
3. AOU
4. LMN
5. OPI
6. FEN
7. TOI
8. SER
9. TTR
10. SES

❋ Solution on page 197 ❋

TWO SUMS

Holmes took a sip of tea. "Fancy an abstract challenge, Watson?"

To be entirely honest, that sort of question tended to fill me with a formless dread. But, knowing it was undoubtedly a useful exercise, I replied that I was prepared to give it a try.

"Excellent," he replied. "Take the digits from 1 to 9, specifically omitting 6. That gives you eight digits. Group those sequentially into numbers of your choice – say 1, 23, 457, 8 and 9, for example – in such a way that you can divide these into two sets of numbers each containing four digits. In our example's case, that could be 1 and 457, and 23, 8 and 9. The trick is to have the sum of your two sets of numbers be the same. 1 + 457 clearly does not equal 23 + 8 + 9." He paused, while my brain reeled a little. "Before you ask, no, you are not allowed to rotate the 9 to turn it into a 6."

"Such a thought never occurred to me," I protested.

"No? Ah well. Anyhow, once you find the answer, if you feel like an extra challenge, try to do the same with the digits forming non-sequential numbers, such as 72 or 814."

Can you find the solution? You are perfectly at leisure to stop after the sequential-digit answer, if you wish.

✷ Solution on page 197 ✷

DUCK DUCK GOOSE

The Peculiar Case of the Raven Child took Holmes and I to the Dysynni Valley. Whilst much of what we encountered there was odd to say the least, there was at least a horrible logic to it, at least when examined after the fact.

The same could not be said of a sign we saw outside one farmer's cottage. "Two chickens for a duck; three chickens and a duck for two geese," it declared, in wild handwriting. In smaller, neater lettering beneath, there was a further offer: "Three geese, one chicken and two ducks for 25 shillings. NO CHANGE."

"Eccentric fellow," I observed to Holmes.

"Probably spent the night alone on the top of Cader Idris," he replied. "Still, there's enough information there to work out the price of a duck, if you assume his 'no change' means that each bird costs a whole number of shillings."

Can you work out the value of a duck?

✳ Solution on page 198 ✳

THE JEWELLER

During *The Adventure of the Impossible Gecko*, we had reason to examine the movements of a certain jeweller of Hatton Gardens, a fellow named Stewartson. The Baker Street Irregulars were despatched to keep an eye on his movements, particularly with regards to the timing of his journey to and from work.

When Wiggins reported back to us, he informed us that Stewartson often took a handsome cab to and from work, and on those occasions, his total journey time to and from his shop was 30 minutes. On some mornings, however, he walked into work, and then caught a cab home when he finished. On those occasions, his total journey time was one and a half hours.

I made some comment to the effect that Wiggins could just have told us how long it took the fellow to walk to work, and Holmes archly replied that he'd done just that.

How long was Stewartson's walk to work?

✳ Solution on page 198 ✳

THE NOTE

Holmes had been tinkering away in his study for the best part of a couple of hours, testing a range of pungent chemical experiments, when he came out bearing a purple-speckled notebook.

———❖———

"Take a look at this, old chap," he said, and passed it over.

I took the notebook, and was about to examine it when Holmes turned on his heel and returned to the study. "Let me know when you've cracked it," he said, before closing the door.

Mystified, I opened the book, trying to avoid the purple splotches. The front page was the only one to bear any writing, and its contents were these:

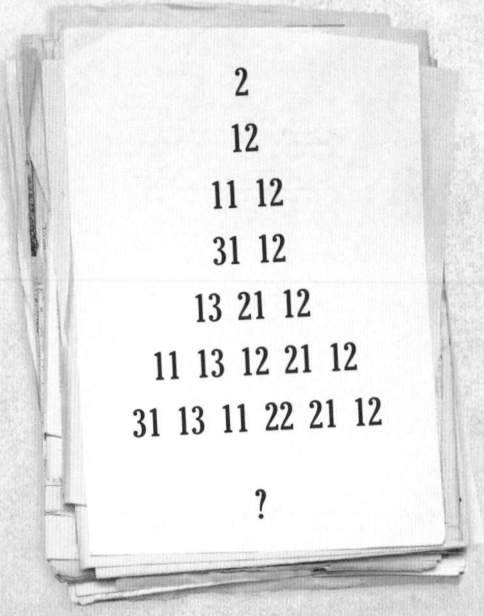

2

12

11 12

31 12

13 21 12

11 13 12 21 12

31 13 11 22 21 12

?

What should the next line be?

✳ Solution on page 198 ✳

SERPENTINE

Holmes and I were sitting in Hyde Park on a pleasant Sunday afternoon, watching people boating on the river. Specifically, we were watching Alice Mills and her beau, Gabriel Sieger. Thus far, Miss Mills had done nothing particularly noteworthy, but it was a reasonably diverting way of spending an afternoon.

"You know, I assume, that a boat, floating, displaces a certain amount of water," Holmes said, conversationally.

I nodded.

"You also know, I trust, that the weight of the water displaced is equal to the weight of the boat."

I nodded again, wondering where he was going.

"It follows then that Miss Mills and Mr Sieger together will have raised the level of the water a small amount when they got into the boat, which we can assume was already afloat."

"I suppose so," I said.

"So what would happen to the level of the water if Mr Sieger fell out of the boat, and those counterfeiter's plates in his jacket sank him to the floor of the Serpentine like a stone?"

❋ Solution on page 198 ❋

THE LEGACY

I remember reading in the *Evening Standard* of an instance where an old soldier died childless, and left his modest bequest to his nephews, Ronald and Frederick. It was just below a silly story about a Canadian poltergeist. The piece was of interest only because of the somewhat tangled way in which the deceased had specified the money be divided. The newspaper took a humorous slant on the story, playing up the perplexity of the lawyer involved, and painting the dead man as an enthusiastic prankster. The truth of these claims is left to your personal judgement regarding the veracity of newspaper reporters.

———————

However editorialized the story might have been, the base facts were that the fellow left £100 precisely, and determined the allotment of inheritance by saying that subtracting a third of Ronald's legacy from a quarter of Frederick's would give a difference of £11.

How much did Ronald get?

✳ Solution on page 199 ✳

CHILDREN

Having brought up some breakfast for Holmes and myself, Mrs Hudson rather spoiled my appetite by informing us that her cousin Davey and his wife were trying vigorously for a family. Whilst I was still attempting to get rid of the mental images thus conjured, she continued by saying, "They've decided they'd like to have four children, nice and quickly."

As a doctor, I naturally found the idea of both "nice" and "quickly" being applied to four pregnancies to be somewhat implausible, but I held my peace.

Mrs Hudson continued blithely on. "They're hoping not to get all four children the same sex. The real question, of course, is whether they're more likely to have two of each, or three of one."

"I'm sure the good Doctor could answer that for you," Holmes said, arching an eyebrow in my direction. "Assuming that they're equally likely to have a boy or a girl each time."

"Oh, yes," said Mrs Hudson. "Thank you, Doctor." I'm sure I saw her suppressing a mischievous grin.

Can you work out the answer?

❋ Solution on page 199 ❋

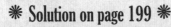

THE REVENGE

Edward Blaydon was the captain of the *Revenge*, an ill-aspected sloop that claimed Cape Town as its home berth. This was during *The Adventure of the Sapphire Gin*, and a very strange affair it was too. Holmes had lured Blaydon to a luncheon in St. James', where we met him in the guise of shady exporters to ostensibly discuss the transport of a cargo from Whitby to Varna, on the Bulgarian coast.

"I know the Black Sea like the back of my hand," Blaydon said confidently. "I can get your merchandise into Varna, no questions asked, and that's a guarantee. I'll do it in under a week, too."

"That sounds very promising," Holmes replied. "Are you certain that your ship is up to the task?"

"The *Revenge*? Ha. Of course. I admit that it's not much to look at, but that's one of the fastest packet-runners you'll find in any of London's docks."

Holmes nodded thoughfully. "I noticed that you're registered in Cape Town. Is that where you're from?"

"Where's any seaman from, Mr Gordon?" Gordon was Holmes. I was going by Hendricks. "I belong to the oceans. Ports are just places where you buy booze, food, and other little niceties. I'm a Portsmouth lad, originally. But I've spent my time in the shadow of Table Mountain, if that's what's worrying you."

A little while later, we took our leave with some vague promises and assurances. As soon as we were out of the restaurant, Holmes shook his head disapprovingly. "I assume that you realized our friend was no sailor, Watson? Anyone hearing him would have."

What did he mean?

✳ Solution on page 199 ✳

THE TRUNK

Holmes and I were walking along a sleepy lane in Hookland, making our way back to the inn at which we had secured lodgings after scouting out the estates of the supposed major, C. L. Nolan. Up ahead, a tractor was slowly pulling a chained tree trunk along the lane. Fortunately it had been trimmed of its branches, but it was still an imposing sight.

When we'd overtaken the thing, Holmes surprised me by turning sharply on his heel and walking back along the trunk. I stopped where I was to watch him. He continued at a steady pace until he'd passed the last of it, then reversed himself once more, and walked back to me.

"Come along, old chap," he said as he walked past.

Shaking my head, I duly followed.

"It took me 140 paces to walk from the back of the tree to the front, and just twenty to walk from the front to the back," he declared.

"Well of course," I said. "The tree was moving, after all."

"Precisely," he said. "My pace is one yard in length, so how long is that tree-trunk?"

Can you find the answer?

❋ Solution on page 200 ❋

THE FIELD

One of the side effects of our trip to Hookland was that for several days thereafter, Holmes was given to couching his little mental exercises for me in agricultural terms. I suppose it did make something of a change to be considering matters pastoral rather than, say, fiscal or horological. There was something a little odd about it, however. Either way, it came to an end when *The Adventure of the Wandering Bishops* did.

As a practical example, consider this problem that Holmes set me during that period. There is a particular field which three of a farmer's animals – a cow, a goat, and a lamb – are set to graze. If it were just the cow and the goat, they would graze it bare in 45 days. Without the cow, the goat and the lamb will consume all the grass in 90 days. Absent the goat, the cow and lamb will eat all the pasture in 60 days. The farmer, however, has turned all three loose in the field. How long will it take the three combined to graze out the field?

You may assume for the sake of simplicity that the growth of the grass is irrelevant.

✳ Solution on page 200 ✳

THE TYPE

During *The Adventure of the Third Carriage*, we spent some time talking to a printer. Holmes was after some nugget of information, but felt that the matter needed to be addressed obliquely, so we spent more than an hour with the fellow.

He was nice enough, as printers go, but he was somewhat fixated on a batch of calendars that had been commissioned from him. They were of the style of one month to a page, and had to be printed in a very specific – and expensively ornate – typeface. Because of this, the man was keen to minimize the number of movable type letters that he had to purchase.

He was quite proud of himself for having found the thriftiest solution that would allow him to print the names of the months in full. Using all capital letters was part of it, of course, but the main portion involved ensuring that he had just enough individual letters to assemble any given month.

Can you work out how many letters he had to purchase?

STABBING

"It was the butler who found my father on the floor of the study, Mr Holmes." Emma Porter was a pleasant-seeming woman in her late twenties, her face heavily scored with grief. "He actually stumbled over the body in the darkness. The fire had gone out, you see. His shrieks woke the maid and myself up."

"Did you have any reason to suspect your father was in danger?" Holmes kept his voice politely neutral in tone.

"No, of course not. I mean, he had to lay a fellow off yesterday, and he had a rival or two, but who would stoop to brutal murder over chauffeuring?" Her eyes welled with tears.

"Why did he sack that chap?"

"Drinking," she said. "At least, that's what I understood."

Holmes frowned slightly. "Did he ever drive clients around himself?"

"Almost never, but perhaps if he was desperately short-staffed he might have. He generally kept himself distant from the drivers."

"I see," Holmes said. "And he was found dead shortly after midnight."

"That's right," she said. "The butler was on his way to bed, but noticed that father was on the floor as he passed the study. I had been asleep for some hours by that point. The maid would have been in bed by eleven, too. All the windows were closed, of course. The police said that he'd been stabbed repeatedly. It just doesn't make sense." She folded inward on herself gently.

"I'm confident we'll find the answers very soon," Holmes said. "We already have our primary suspect."

Who does Holmes suspect, and why?

✳ Solution on page 201 ✳

BALANCE

One morning, I observed Holmes rolling a shilling back and forth over his knuckles, from one finger to the next, with his other hand held behind his back. "You can do a lot of mischief with a tricked coin, old friend," he said.

———————◆◆◆———————

"That looks real enough to me," I replied.

"This? Oh, it is. But surely you have heard of gamblers' coins that are cunningly weighted to favour heads over tails, or vice versa?"

I allowed that I had indeed.

"Such devices are a nasty trap for the unwary. But it is possible to get a totally unbiased either/or result from any weighted coin."

"Oh?"

"Indeed. Can you tell me how?"

Can you work it out?

❋ Solution on page 201 ❋

THE MANAGER

Once the safety of the frightened carpenter was assured, and the tome located to a reasonable degree of safety (if not actually recovered), Holmes and I had occasion to speak to a rather evasive little warehouse manager and his somewhat apologetic deputy. The deputy was clearly of better character, so whilst I distracted the manager with some discussion of high-grade medical steel, Holmes chatted to the younger man.

Later, as we departed, Holmes told me a curious thing. The deputy, he said, confessed to Holmes that he had actually enquired about his boss's age a few days beforehand. He was told that the manager was twice as old as the deputy had been, back when the manager had been the same age as the deputy now was.

We already knew from our researches that the manager was 48. How old did that make the deputy?

❋ Solution on page 202 ❋

GETTING AHEAD

Flicking through a book of European history, I came across a rather odd account, which I shared with Holmes.

"According to this text, which I admit is somewhat sensationalized, during the French revolution, the locals of Nîmes used to wager on the sizes of the severed heads of nobles and other supposed enemies of the revolution. The task was to estimate how large the head would be once it had been dipped in wax, but before it had been set out for display. People would bring along vegetables, sometimes carefully trimmed, which they felt would best match the head of a particular condemned person. The closest guess won the pot."

"Ingenious and enterprising," Holmes replied. "Thoroughly French."

"It seems like the very devil of a thing to judge," I said.

"Really?" Holmes sounded amused. "Can you not think of a simple way to get a precise verdict?"

✳ Solution on page 202 ✳

BICYCLE

I noticed Holmes looking distracted one morning over breakfast, tossing a piece of toast into the air before catching it again, over and over like a cat with a toy.

"Something on your mind, old man?" I asked him.

"The valencies of sulphur," he replied. "Particularly in the way that they relate to its propensity to form astringents with zinc."

"Ah," I replied.

"Here's something mostly unrelated for you to chew over, my dear Watson. Say you and I have a single bicycle between us, and no other transport options save walking. We want to get the both of us to a location eighteen miles distant as swiftly as possible. If my walking speed is five miles per hour compared to your four, but for some reason – perhaps a bad ligament – my cycling speed is eight miles per hour compared to your ten. How would you get us simultaneously to our destination with maximum rapidity?"

"A cab," I suggested.

"Without cheating," Holmes replied, and went back to tossing his toast in the air.

✳ Solution on page 203 ✳

THE CANVAS

"Let us say that I needed to paint a very particular picture," Holmes said to me one afternoon.

"I would find such a proposition alarming, given your utter absence of any previously displayed artistic talent."

"You do me a disservice," Holmes replied. "But that is not important. This painting needs to occupy precisely 72 square inches, and measure a whole number of inches on each side. Furthermore, it needs to have a clear border of exactly four inches above and below, and two inches to either side."

"That is quite specific," I observed.

"Very much so," he said. "What is the smallest canvas I could fit such a painting on?"

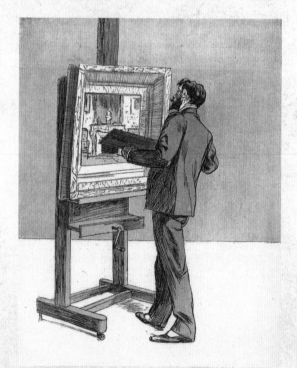

✷ Solution on page 203 ✷

PIG

In Hookland, Holmes and I discovered that the elusive C. L. Nolan had made a suspiciously large purchase of livestock. Converting all the assorted value to shillings for simplicity, he bought pigs at 95s each, and sheep at 97s each, for a grand total of 4,238s – well over two hundred pounds sterling. The dealer who furnished us with this information was still somewhat dazed by the entire transaction. About the only other pieces of information that we got out of the fellow were that Nolan paid entirely in crown coins of all things, and that he would somehow arrange for the livestock to be transported to a number of destinations over the next few weeks.

It was very peculiar, which honestly rather matches my overall opinion of Hookland as a county.

As we left the dealer, Holmes said to me, "So how many pigs did he purchase?"

It was late that night before I could furnish him with an answer. Can you find one?

✳ Solution on page 204 ✳

THE SEVENTH WORDKNOT

I received my seventh slip of wordknot paper from Holmes as we were bouncing down the horribly uneven streets of Bethnal Green in a cab. At the time, it seemed all too plausible that the driver's mind had been seized by fiends or, at the very least, some esoteric specimen of mental disturbance. Holmes had clearly been waiting for precisely such an occasion, for he whipped out the note with a delighted flourish, and presented it to me.

———◆——◆——◆———

I received it with lamentable ill grace. On it were the usual ten lines of three jumbled letters, each row being formed by taking one letter from each of three ten-letter words, starting with the three initial letters on the first row, and proceeding regularly to the ten final letters on the tenth row. The task of unpicking the three loosely themed ten-letter words was not helped by my ongoing fear of imminent disaster, nor by my fight to prevent my breakfast from attempting escape.

The rows of letters were as follows:

1. DPM
2. IOI
3. CUS
4. HAN
5. TOR
6. NEE
7. EBS
8. SAQ
9. TUN
10. KEY

Can you find the words?

✳ Solution on page 205 ✳

THE SHOPKEEPER

Whilst browsing in a shop one dreary afternoon, I overheard the following conversation taking place between a shopkeeper and a neatly dressed gentleman of advancing years. At the time, it made perfect sense, but on reflection, it occurs to me that it might be an amusing test.

"What would it cost me for just one?" the gentleman asked.

"Two shillings," came the reply.

The customer nodded. "So that means twelve would cost...?"

"Four shillings," the shopkeeper said, keeping his voice carefully patient.

"That's very good," the customer replied. "I'll take three hundred and twelve then, please."

"Of course, sir." The shopkeeper started collecting items for the customer. "Six shillings, please."

What was the gentleman purchasing?

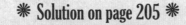

❋ Solution on page 205 ❋

MATCH TWO

As Holmes put it when setting me this challenge, "You may find that a bit of mechanical aid proves of assistance with this one, my dear Watson." In other words, get some tooth-picks or matches.

The task is, using matches, to remove seven-tenths of five and in so doing, leave exactly four remaining.

It is quite obvious when you know how it is done, but to be frank, I did struggle for a while with this one. Holmes was quite steadfast in refusing me any sort of hint, and merely sat there, poring through a rather sensationalist volume of criminal activity that had taken place in Leeds over the past few years. From what little I saw of it, it must have been depressing reading. Not, of course, that I should wish to give the impression I that I am singling Leeds out as especially criminal; merely that Holmes' interest in crime was entirely catholic.

Anyhow, Leeds is by the by. Can you find the solution?

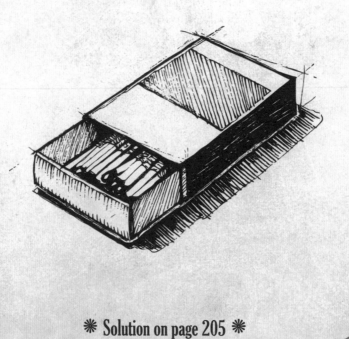

✳ Solution on page 205 ✳

CURIO

"I have a little mathematical curio for you," Holmes told me one afternoon.

---✦◆✦---

I eyed him warily. "Oh?"

"There are two separate pairs of numbers between one and nine which, when each is squared, and these squares are added to the product of multiplying the numbers together, give you a total which is also a square. Can you identify one of the pairs?"

"Let me just straighten that out," I told him. "Two different single-digit numbers, no zeroes. Multiply them by each other, and by themselves. Add the three totals together, and get a square number. Find one of two solutions."

"Precisely so," Holmes said. "There are only 81 pairs, if you don't fancy tackling the algebra."

Can you solve the problem?

✳ Solution on page 206 ✳

SIX FEET UNDER

Holmes and I were walking across the Regent's Park on our way back to 221b, having just sorted out the unpleasant *Affair of the Maida Vale baker*. It was 13 June, a date which sticks in my mind for reasons that will swiftly become quite clear. We were just passing the nursery when Holmes glanced over at the blooming flower beds, and bade me stop. I did so immediately, alert for any sign of pursuit.

"We're almost to the longest day of the year," he proclaimed. "We sit on the very cusp of spring and summer. Agreed?"

I nodded, mildly bemused.

"So tell me then, Watson. What season is it, ten feet straight down?"

✳ Solution on page 206 ✳

ENGINE TROUBLE

It is a long haul from Bangor to London by train, particularly when your route requires several changes. The Dysynni Valley is beautiful, in a stark sense, but it's a devil of a haul from Baker Street. Our journey back was not helped by an engine problem that one of the trains on our route developed.

———◆◈◆———

We'd been on this particular leg of the journey for an hour when our speed was suddenly cut to three-fifths of its former magnitude. Consequently, we were two hours late arriving at our destination, and missed our connection.

The guard did apologise on behalf of the driver, and informed us that if the problem had developed 50 miles later, we would have arrived 40 minutes sooner, and made our connection. This was not any great comfort.

Can you calculate how long this particular leg of the journey was?

✳ Solution on page 207 ✳

RECALL

Memory is a curious thing. I recall a conversation with Holmes on the matter, where he proposed that there were in fact many different forms of memory – immediate, autobiographical, muscular, visual, audial, linguistic, and more – and that different people would often have varied facilities in these areas. Certainly, I knew a fellow with a very sharp memory, who could recall a snatch of song or read passage from a decade ago with perfect alacrity, but had genuine trouble recalling what he'd done the day before, and had to work his birthday out by starting with the current date.

At the conclusion of the discussion, Holmes proceeded to test my immediate memory with a rather confusing little mental calculation.

"Tell me," he said, "what is the number which when tripled, and this product increased by seventy five percent, the result divided by seven, the quotient reduced by a third, the result multiplied by itself, this square reduced by fifty-two, the square root found of this remaining difference, this root added to eight, and the sum divided by ten, results in the number two?"

Luckily, I have good short-term recall. You have the advantage of being able to refer back to the problem.

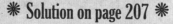
✳ Solution on page 207 ✳

MORAN

As you may be aware, Holmes and I on occasion tangled with an extremely lethal fellow by the name of Colonel Moran. Holmes believed him to be the second most dangerous man in London at one time, and was almost certainly correct.

One of the incidents which led Moran to leave the army was a disagreement over a brutal firearm that he had personally invented. There was a call at the time for improved weapons, with a substantial purse waiting for people who could match the stringent requirements. Moran put forth a repeating rifle which, he said, would fire 60 shots at the rate of one every five seconds.

It is true that the assessing panel, who were men of good character, were ill-disposed to accept Moran's petition. Even then, he had the reputation of a brutal, nigh-uncontrollable monster. Still, they had technicians test the device. The panel accepted that Moran's gun took five minutes to fire 60 shots, and then rejected the rifle on the grounds that it did not live up to his claims. Moran was incandescent, and within six months, had become a career criminal specializing in assassination and card-sharping.

Was the panel's assessment of failure accurate?

❋ Solution on page 208 ❋

THE EIGHTH WORDKNOT

You are probably familiar with Mr Joseph Paxton's glittering masterpiece, the Crystal Palace. Holmes and I were within its glass confines one afternoon. A fellow by the name of Andrew Hodder was going to be within the Alhambran Court, and for several reasons, Holmes felt it wise to observe him.

Mr Hodder duly arrived, and swiftly took a seat, then started sketching. After a minute or so, Holmes decided that Hodder was clearly going to be some time, and handed me the paper on which was recorded the eighth wordknot. As on previous occasions, this took the form of ten rows of three letters, thus:

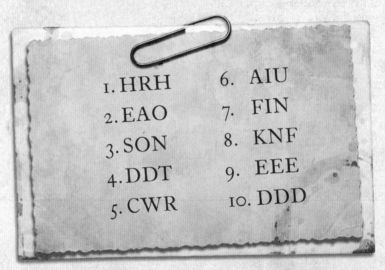

1. HRH
2. EAO
3. SON
4. DDT
5. CWR
6. AIU
7. FIN
8. KNF
9. EEE
10. DDD

Three loosely related ten-letter words were obscured within, their first letters on the first row, their second letters on the second row, and so on. My task, which I hand down to you, was to unravel the three words.

Can you find the solution?

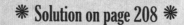

✳ Solution on page 208 ✳

BARNABAS

We met up with Wiggins one fine spring morning to find him in particularly high spirits. When we enquired, he explained that he'd helped an ageing gardener of his acquaintance to dig a client's ditch the afternoon before, for which he had been handsomely paid.

"He tried to give me three half-crowns," Wiggins said, sounding slightly awed. "Said it was what he'd be paid for the ditch, and as I'd done most of the work, and helped him out of a spot besides, I could take it all. I only took what was fair, though. Greed is bad for business, and this way maybe he'll have me help out some other time."

"Very admirable," I told him. "What was your fair share?"

Wiggins grinned, and winked at Holmes. "Thought you'd ask me that, Doctor. Look at it this way. Old Barnabas was able to dig as rapidly as I could shovel the loose dirt out of the trench, but I could dig four times as fast as he could shovel out dirt. It's not that either of us was worse at shovelling than at digging, you understand. It's just slower. The effort rate is the same. So you tell me, what do you think is fair?"

It took me a while to find an answer. Can you do so?

✳ Solution on page 208 ✳

THE FORTY-FOUR

Mrs Hudson seemed out of sorts. It was nothing that I could immediately put my finger on, but something was amiss.

I offered her a smile. "Are you feeling quite alright, Mrs Hudson?"

She sighed. "I'm fine, Doctor. Thank you. I'm concerned about my uncle Michael. I saw him on Sunday for the first time in several years. He lives down on the Lizard now, you know, in Cornwall. At one point the conversation turned to age, and I asked him how old my cousin Minnie was now. He fell silent for a moment, and then told me that she was 1,280 years old! Then he corrected himself, and said that she was 44. But her older brother Douglas was 40 last year. I got to the root of it in the end – he first multiplied her age with his own, and then subtracted hers from it. I'm afraid his mind is going."

"I'm dreadfully sorry to hear that," I told her. "It's a terrible business."

She thanked me, and carried on. After she'd left, I found myself pondering the ages of Minnie and her father. Can you work them out?

✳ Solution on page 209 ✳

THE MURDER OF MOLLY GLASS

The death of Molly Glass seemed like a tragic suicide. The woman in question, who was married and in her thirties, but childless, was found dead inside her bedroom. The room contained a gas fire, connected to the mains, as is so common nowadays. The gas was switched on, but unlit, and this was most definitely the cause of death. Post-mortem indicators made this perfectly plain. The windows of the bedroom were firmly closed, and latched from the inside. They were unbroken and undisturbed. The bedroom door was also locked from the inside, and there were no other means of egress.

Mrs Glass's mother was most insistent that her daughter would never have taken her own life, and refused to believe the police's complacent insistence on suicide. The lack of any sort of note did certainly encourage the possibility of such speculation. And so the case duly came before Holmes. He glanced at the details, and then tossed them aside declaring that it was clearly murder, that her husband was mostly likely the culprit, and that his expertise was needed no further in the matter.

He was, of course, correct in all points. But how was it done?

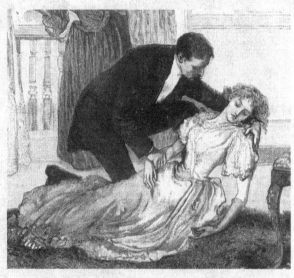

✳ Solution on page 209 ✳

FIENDISH PUZZLES

PIPE DREAMS

Whilst I was serving in the army, I spent some time in Afghanistan, and there I came across a curious treatise that had been translated into English. The document, entitled *The Red Tower,* claimed to be the work of one Ghirgiz al-Uqbar, a name that suggested a non-local origin. It was a highly whimsical piece, but one section in particular is worth recalling for my current purposes.

———◆◆◆———

In this section, the author decries the even population balance between men and women, suggesting that there ought to be more women, so that harems could be larger. From this highly dubious suggestion, he goes on to state that if he were ruler, he would pass an edict that required a woman to stop having children if and only if she had a son. Thus, he reasoned, families would have many daughters but just one son, and in a score of years, there would be a surfeit of unmarried young women.

His plan was clearly insane, but do you think it would have worked, if somehow implemented rigorously?

❋ Solution on page 212 ❋

THE OLD ONES

A curious incident in Bethnal Green came to my attention one Tuesday morning, in the *Evening Standard*. A fellow walked into a pub on the Cambridge Heath road, and asked the man behind the bar for a glass of water. The response was immediate – the man pulled out a gun, and immediately shot the would-be customer dead.

Unfortunately for the murderer, there was a witness he was unaware of, one of the regular serving girls. She escaped detection, and was able to describe the day's horror to the police. She was also able to confirm that the murderer did not appear to have known the victim or harbour any sort of grudge against him, but also did not seem to be killing simply for the dark joy of it. According to the newspaper, the police even mentioned that the victim had not had hiccups.

Can you find the reason why this murder happened?

✳ Solution on page 212 ✳

RIFLE ROUNDS

Whilst in Afghanistan, I stumbled across the odd fact that rifle shells were packed in boxes of fifteen, eighteen or twenty shells. This piqued my interest, so during a quiet moment, I sought out a quartermaster to enquire as to the reasoning behind it.

"It's so they can send out exactly as many shells as a dump needs without having to muck around with breaking open a box," the man told me.

"Surely that can't work," I said. "What if you wanted seven shells? Or 29?"

"What dump is ever going to want just seven shells?" replied the quartermaster. "Yes, alright, there are some low numbers where it breaks down, and you have to send more, but for the vast majority of orders, it's just fine. Anything over a certain threshold will work, you know."

Can you calculate what that threshold might be?

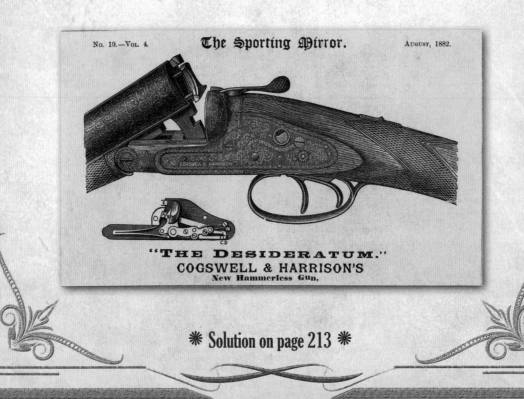

No. 19.—Vol. 4.   The Sporting Mirror.   August, 1882.

"THE DESIDERATUM."
COGSWELL & HARRISON'S
New Hammerless Gun,

✳ Solution on page 213 ✳

THE PLEASANT WAY

During *The Peculiar Case of the Raven Child*, Holmes and I had cause to examine the movements of a suspicious fellow named Rowlands. I won't bore you with the specifics of the intrigue here, but one morning, Rowlands set out to walk over the hills from Tywyn to another town a modest distance away. At precisely the same time, his acquaintance Jones left Rowlands's destination, heading for Tywyn.

Their movements were notably suspicious. The pair met briefly at the point ten miles from Tywyn. Spending identical amounts of time in their destinations, they set off on their return journeys in such a manner that they met again, this time twelve miles from Jones' original starting point. Their walking speeds, of course, were consistent throughout.

How far apart are the two towns?

✳ Solution on page 213 ✳

FASHION

On one occasion, Holmes and I were asked to solve the robbery of a number of dresses from the workshop of a recently deceased ladies' tailor to the upper echelons of society. Holmes took a short look at the particulars of the case, and sent them all back to the gown-maker's son with a scribbled note to the effect that it could only be one particular seamstress, with the help of her husband.

However, glancing through my observations some period later, I observed certain facts about the robbery which led me to an interesting little exercise. The stock at the workshop had been very recently valued at the princely sum of £1,800, and when examined after the theft, comprised of precisely 100 completed dresses in a range of styles, but of equal valuation. However, there was no remaining record of how many dresses had been there beforehand. The son did recall his father stating, of the valuation, that if he'd had thirty dresses more, then a valuation of £1,800 would have meant £3 less per dress.

Are you able to calculate how many dresses were stolen?

✳ Solution on page 213 ✳

THE FOURTH CAMOUFLAGE

I'd just scalded the roof of my mouth on a surprisingly hot spoonful of Scots porridge one morning when Holmes decided to seize the moment and throw one of his camouflaged word puzzles at me. The words he called out to me were stonecutter, tardigrades, cassowaries and matrimonial.

—◆◆◆—

I knew from bitter experience that Holmes would not repeat the words, so made an effort to memorize them whilst simultaneously attempting to resist the urge to yell aloud at the pain in my mouth.

The task, as ever, was to discover the four smaller words, one within each of the longer, that were united by a common theme.

Can you do it? I recommend not burning yourself in the mouth before beginning. It is not helpful.

✳ Solution on page 214 ✳

THE APPLE MARKET

We stumbled across a practical instance of this odd little puzzler whilst in Hookland. Rather than try to replicate our experience exactly, however, I shall endeavour to abstract it slightly, so that it is easier to see to the heart of the matter. Hookland, as I have mentioned earlier, is a strange county.

———◆◆◆———

The market held a group of three apple-sellers, friends with different species of apples to sell, and thus different prices. One of the ladies sold her apples at two for a penny, the second at three for a penny, and the third at five for tuppence. Around 11 a.m., however, both of the first two ladies had to suddenly depart. Each had 30 apples remaining. These 60 were handed to the remaining friend, who proceeded to sell them at her usual price of five for two pence.

If the two missing ladies had stayed to sell their stock, they would have brought in 25 pence between them. Now three apples at one penny and two apples at one penny together clearly equals five apples for tuppence. However, when the third lady sold her friends' stock, she brought in only 24 pence, as 60 divided by five is twelve, and split that evenly between her friends.

So where did the odd penny get to?

❋ Solution on page 214 ❋

A PAIR OF FOURS

Holmes took a puff on his pipe. "You are familiar, I trust, my dear Watson, with the principle of expressing a whole number in terms of a different number plus some mathematical operators."

I nodded. "Such as four being two times two, you mean."

"Precisely. And 63 being two to the power of two times two plus two, with two divided by two subtracted from it."

I jotted $(2\char`^(2*2+2))-2/2$ down on a notepad, resolved it to $(2\char`^6)-1 = 64-1 = 63$, and nodded again.

"Capital," Holmes said. "So can you likewise find a way of expressing 64 using as many mathematical operators as you like, but only two instances of the digit 4, and no other digits? It may take you a little time."

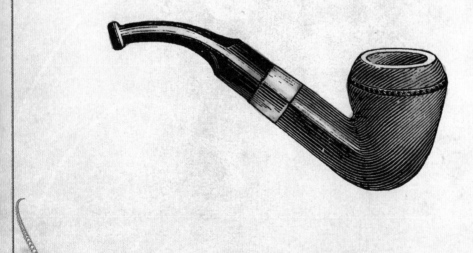

✳ Solution on page 214 ✳

ASHCOURT STATION

As I know all too well, it takes five hours to get from Ashcourt to London Waterloo – or back, for that matter. Trains leave every hour, on the hour, in both directions. Holmes and I were on the Waterloo train, heading back to London with a certain amount of relief. Some time after our departure, a train rattled past in the other direction, heading into Ashcourt.

"More poor devils heading into Hookland," I observed.

"They're not the last we'll see," said Holmes absentmindedly.

"No," I said, although now I think about it, using a negative to indicate agreement does seem slightly farcical. Versatile language we have.

"In fact, Watson," Holmes said, "Why don't you tell me how many Waterloo-to-Ashcourt trains will pass us on our way?"

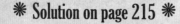

✳ Solution on page 215 ✳

ANDREW

Holmes and I have encountered many highly peculiar individuals over the years. One of the most singular, however, was a fellow by the name of Andrew who was caught up in *The Adventure of the Black Alchemist*. Despite a certain preoccupation with fried-egg sandwiches, he was a quick-witted and resourceful fellow, and his heart was in the right place, both metaphorically and medically.

I vividly remember him explaining to Holmes and myself that he had lost his pocket watch in a scuffle with a cloaked and hooded figure whom he suspected of being an occultist. He went on to explain that on occasions when he forgot to wind his carriage clock at home, he would rectify the problem by visiting his friend David, who somehow always anticipated his arrival. Then he'd spend the evening there, and return home, correctly setting his clock when he arrived back.

It occurred to me that this must be rather haphazard, as he had no way of precisely telling the duration of the return trip, but he countered that as long as it took as long going there as he did getting back, it didn't matter.

What was his method?

✻ Solution on page 215 ✻

CENTURIAL

One afternoon, Mrs Hudson rather unexpectedly provided Holmes and myself with a slice of Victoria sponge cake each to go with our teas.

———◆———

"Is it a special occasion, Mrs Hudson?" I enquired.

"Indeed it is, Doctor. Indeed it is."

I smiled. "Oh, well –"

"Yes, my cousin Jack and his sons total precisely 100 years of age between them today," she said proudly. "Further more, Jack is exactly twice the age of his oldest son, who is himself twice the age of the middle son, who is twice the age of the youngest son. Quite the unique occurrence."

"Ah," I managed. "Yes. Congratulations are in order."

She beamed at me.

Once she'd gone, Holmes turned to me. "Further congratulations will be in order if you can tell me precisely how old Jack is today."

Can you find the answer?

✳ Solution on page 215 ✳

ROCK PAPER SCISSORS

Wiggins grinned at me. "You've not played Rock Paper Scissors before, Doctor?"

"Doesn't ring a bell," I told him.

"Two of you randomly pick one of the three, and shout your choice simultaneously. There are hand gestures, too. If you both get the same, it's a draw. Otherwise, scissors beats paper, paper beats rock, and rock beats scissors."

"So it's a way of settling an argument," I suggested.

"You were brought up wrong, Doctor," Wiggins said gravely. "Look, try it this way. I played a series of ten games with Alice earlier. I picked scissors six times, rock three times, and paper once. She picked scissors four time, rock twice, and paper four times. None of our games were drawn." He glanced at Holmes, who nodded. "So then, Doctor. What was the overall score for the series?"

✳ Solution on page 216 ✳

OLD HOOK

An event that occurred during *The Adventure of the Wandering Bishops* inspired Holmes to devise a particularly tricky little mental exercise for my ongoing improvement. There were times when I thoroughly appreciated and enjoyed his efforts, and times when I found them somewhat unwelcome. I'm afraid that this was one of the latter occasions. It had been a bad week.

"Picture three farmers," Holmes told me. "Hooklanders. We'll call them Ern, Ted, and Hob."

"If I must," I muttered.

"It will help," Holmes replied. "Ern has a horse and cart, with an average speed of eight mph. Ted can walk just one mph, given his bad knee, and Hob is a little better at two mph, thanks to his back."

"A fine shower," I said. "Can't I imagine them somewhat fitter?"

"Together, these worthies want to go from Old Hook to Coreham, a journey of 40 miles. So Ern got Ted in his cart, drove him most of the way, and dropped him off to walk the rest. Then he went back to get Hob, and took him into Coreham, arriving exactly as Ted did. How long did the journey take?"

Can you find a solution?

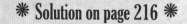

✳ Solution on page 216 ✳

ART

One of my medical patients came to see me with a sore arm, but he seemed far more interested in his financial situation than his medical one. It can be that way for some people, particularly men in my experience – aversion to considering unpleasant medical possibilities leads them to emphatic fixation on something utterly unrelated. The fellow just had a light sprain, but that didn't stop him rabbiting on about some art dealing he'd been attempting.

Despite my best attempts otherwise, he resolutely insisted on informing me that he'd sold two paintings the day before, each for £75. One of these produced a 25 per cent profit, but the other yielded a 25 per cent loss.

I informed him absent-mindedly that it could have been worse.

"Not at all," he replied. "It was a very bad day."

I back-pedalled a little to avoid offence, and told him I was referring to his arm. But do you know what he was talking about?

✳ **Solution on page 217** ✳

DAISY

Mrs Hudson was collecting teacups from our rooms, and tutting to herself at the various places where the blessed things had ended up. When she hit a round dozen cups, she let out an enormous sigh, and turned to me.

———◆◆———

"Have I mentioned my cousin Daisy?" she asked.

"Not that I recall, Mrs Hudson," I said.

"She's had two children so far. One of them is a boy."

I fought to keep my bemusement off my face. "Oh?"

"How probable do you think it is that the other is a girl?"

Across the room, Holmes chuckled.

Can you find the answer?

✳ **Solution on page 217** ✳

THE NINTH WORDKNOT

I'd barely blurted the answer to Holmes's devilish two-fours puzzle when he produced a slip of paper with a flourish and a quite evil smirk, and handed that over too. Sure enough, it proved to be one of his wordknots, and a stern one to boot. I looked wistfully out of the window, at the rather fine afternoon I was missing, and set myself back to work.

The paper bore the letters:

1. BTM
2. RUR
3. OES
4. KAB
5. DEU

6. SCT
7. HEW
8. EOE
9. RTR
10. SDS

Each row held one letter from each of three words, jumbled into no particular order. These letters were all from the same position in each word, and presented in correct sequence, so that the first row held the first letters, the second row held the second letters, and so on and so forth. My task, of course, was to discover what the three ten-letter words were. I knew only that they would be loosely related.

✳ Solution on page 217 ✳

THE SEVEN

Mrs Hudson eyed me grudgingly from over her stack of retrieved teacups. "My cousin Daisy took her two and her sister Allie's five to see a Punch and Judy show last week," she said.

"Oh, yes, the Neapolitan puppet thing," I replied. Visions of devils, mistresses, and wanton violence floated before my mind's eye. "Is that entirely suitable for children?"

"It is nowadays," she said. "More or less. They apparently enjoyed it anyway, the scamps. But that's not the point. The point is that there are three girls amongst the seven, and four boys, and they sat themselves utterly haphazardly in a row. What do you think that the chance was that the end-spots were both occupied by girls?"

That stopped me in my tracks. Can you work it out?

BRIDGE

The game of bridge is an interesting new Russian spin on that perennial pub favourite, whist. One of the things about it which I find the most curious is its seemingly boundless propensity to end up in the newspaper. It seems nowadays that hardly a week goes by without some mention of it in either the *The Times* or the *Evening Standard*.

The other day, I came across a story about a quartet of bridge players whom had each been dealt all thirteen cards of one suit – a phenomenon known as the "perfect deal".

Dismissing those perfect deals that arise from deliberate tampering or ineffective shuffling, how many such events would you expect to occur nationally over the course of one year?

✳ **Solutions on page 217/218** ✳

THE ENTHUSIAST

Colin White's murder came as a nasty shock to the London chess-playing community, particularly when police let it be known that they suspected that a fellow player. Brian Campbell was one of three men who'd visited White that last day, according to a diary entry from that morning. A fellow player of some repute, he'd often been quite critical of White's eccentricities. In addition to Campbell, another chess-player had paid White a visit, a younger man named Tom Wilton, who was said to rather look up to the deceased. Finally, he'd also had a visit from his cousin, Alan Lloyd, a genial chap with a devout love of fishing. Unfortunately, White had listed the men in alphabetical order, rather than time.

Inspector Lestrade was somewhat beside himself, because, following legal advice, none of the men were prepared to make any sort of statement whatsoever. Holmes agreed to help, and a few hours later, he and I were in the dead man's flat.

"We've kept it as it was," Lestrade told us. "We found him in the sitting room, stabbed."

The room was large and restrained. The big central table held four chess boards, one of them set up with a match in the mid-game. I am no chess expert, but I could tell white was winning handily, dominating the board with a line of major pieces, its bishops immediately either side of a rook. Aside from that, there were some small pieces of Greek statuary, a long shelf of books – on chess, inevitably – and a plain ashtray. I considered that perhaps a game had gone badly astray.

Holmes poked around, examined a couple of books, and then turned to Lestrade. "The identity of the murderer blindingly obvious," he said.

I didn't know what he meant at the time. Do you?

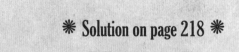

✳ Solution on page 218 ✳

THE FIFTH CAMOUFLAGE

After an unpleasantly long chase through the eastern portion of the City of London, Holmes and I had successfully apprehended a fellow by the name of Raphael Stevens. He was up to his neck in *The Adventure of the Sapphire Gin*, and there were certain pieces of information which we needed from him. Clearly, he had not been willing to speak to us. I was forced to restrain him while Holmes put his questions.

———————

Eventually, we had the knowledge we needed. I let Stevens go, and slumped against a wall, exhausted – which, naturally, was the exact moment when Holmes decided to challenge me with one of his word camouflages.

"Displayable," he said. "Hideosities. Totipotent. Browbeaten."

A groan escaped me. "Really, Holmes?" I asked.

"Crime never waits for your convenience," he said, severely.

So I had to find the answer. Four shorter words, one per longer word, that formed a thematically linked set.

Can you find the theme?

✳ Solution on page 218 ✳

THE RIBBONS

This particular puzzle was another of Holmes's abstract contrivances, inspired, so far as I was ever aware, by a conversation that he had with Mrs Hudson.

The situation is as follows. Four mother and daughter pairs went to purchase ribbon, and over the course of the afternoon, two coincidences could be noted. One was that each mother bought twice as many yards of ribbon as her daughter; the other that each purchaser acquired exactly as many yards of ribbon as the cost of that ribbon per yard in pennies. As examples of that last fact, consider that someone buying one penny a yard ribbon would have purchased one yard, or that someone buying two pence ribbon would have purchased two yards.

In addition to these two foundational coincidences, there are some other pieces of information. Rose purchased two yards more than Daisy. Lily purchased three yards less than Mrs Brown. Mrs White spent 76 pence more than Mrs Black. Daisy spent 48 pence less than Mrs Green.

If Daisy purchased ribbon at four pence a yard, what is Heather's mother named?

✳ Solution on page 219 ✳

BILLY AND JONNY

One Easter Saturday, Mrs Hudson fell to discussing the family members she was expecting to see on the following day. Apparently, it was quite the gathering of the clan, because her recitation lasted quite a while. Unfortunately, she must have noticed that my attention was flagging, along with my good humour, my vital energies, and my will to live.

"Have I mentioned my cousin Trish?" Mrs Hudson asked, after a brief pause.

"Possibly," I said, startled into frankness.

"She has a pair of sons, you know. Billy and Jonny. Apparently, eighteen more than the total of their ages added together comes out at twice Billy's age, whilst six less than the difference between their ages comes out at Jonny's age. What age would that make them?"

Can you find the answer?

❋ Solution on page 219 ❋

TROUT

"There's going to be a number of things on the table for lunch tomorrow," Mrs Hudson told me. "It being Easter and all. My cousin Richard managed to get hold of a lovely trout this morning, so that's going to be poached in a light cream and wine sauce, with chives. There'll be new potatoes to go with it, I'd imagine."

---◆---

"Sounds very pleasant," I ventured.

"I'm sure it will be," she said. "I asked Richard how big the thing was. You know how fishermen love to boast. Well, he only went and told me that the head weighed the same as the combined weight of the tail and half the body, that the body weighed as much as the head and tail together, and that the tail came out at nine ounces. I'm sure you can see what that means."

I kept my own counsel on the implications of that statement, and nodded.

How much does the fish weigh?

✳ Solution on page 219 ✳

GETTING TO MARKET

During our hunt for C. L. Nolan in the course of *The Adventure of the Wandering Bishops*, Holmes and I had to get from Hook, the much-decayed ancient capital town of Hookland, to Coreham, the current capital. In Hookland, they say that Coreham is a cursed city, and there were moments where I felt rather sympathetic to such superstitious claims.

———————◆———————

To our moderate annoyance, the only vehicle available to transport us from Hook to Coreham was a mouldering trap pulled by an equally mouldering old nag. The driver was little better than his conveyance, and showed a remarkable lack of anything resembling sense. Had it not been for a heavy case that Holmes was carrying, we would just have walked. It would have been faster and less aggravating.

After twenty frustratingly slow minutes in the trap, I asked the fellow how far we'd come from Hook.

"Halfways as far as to Doglick from here," mumbled the driver.

I got him to repeat the name, just to be sure I'd heard him correctly. Doglick turned out to be a flyspeck of a hamlet every bit as unprepossessing as its name. Some five miles after we'd got clear of the place, I made the mistake of again asking the driver as to our progress, specifically, how much further it was to Coreham.

His answer, word for word, was identical.

I asked no further questions, and an hour later, we finally arrived in Coreham, which is at least a pretty place.

Can you tell how far it is from Hook to Coreham?

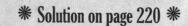

❈ Solution on page 220 ❈

THE TENTH WORDKNOT

Holmes handed me my tenth and final wordknot one quiet afternoon when I was well rested and refreshed, and more than a little bored. I peered at both him and the slip of paper cautiously, half-expecting lions to leap from behind a cupboard the moment I took it from him, or some such terrifying crisis.

———◆◆◆———

As it was, nothing more distressing happened than Holmes smiling at me, which of course unsettled me colossally. The slip of paper bore the following:

1. BAH
2. BAI
3. LOA
4. CCO
5. PET
6. HEN
7. ROY
8. TIS
9. AEI
10. SSL

The task was to unscramble the letters to find three loosely-themed ten-letter words, working from the basis that the first line of the text comprised their initial letters, the second line their second letters, and so on.

It was not easy.

Can you do it?

✳ Solution on page 220 ✳

PENCILS

During *The Adventure of the Third Carriage*, Holmes had the need to spend a day masquerading as a wholesaler of stationery. He returned from this outing much vexed, so naturally I asked him whether his investigations had gone well.

"Oh, yes, very useful," he said. "I got the information I was after."

"But something appears to be bothering you nonetheless," I replied.

He sighed. "The stationery business is cripplingly ineffective. It irks me to have had to pretend to approve of such ridiculous business practices."

"I see," I said. This was not strictly a true or accurate statement.

"Imagine this," Holmes said. "A box of 160 pencils, in eight rows of twenty."

"Sounds about right."

"No!" Holmes sighed again. "You could get ten per cent more pencils to a box in a heartbeat."

Can you see how?

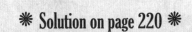

✳ Solution on page 220 ✳

TWO WRONGS

Holmes called me in to his laboratory area one morning. When I got there, curious as to what oddity I might be shown, I discovered that he'd written a very curious equation on the blackboard: WRONG + WRONG = RIGHT.

"You appear to be flying in the face of modern ethics, my dear friend," I told him.

"Appearances can be deceptive," he replied. "This, for example, is a perfectly regular mathematical addition, except that eight of the ten digits from zero to nine have been replaced, in no particular order, with the eight letters that make up the words 'wrong' and 'right'."

"Ingenious," I said.

"Glad you think so, old chap. See if you can find a solution."

Can you do it?

✳ Solution on page 221 ✳

EASTER SPIRIT

Holmes gestured grandly at the coffee table. "There are four eggs," he began.

"I hate to disagree, old chap," I said. "There don't appear to be any eggs there at all."

He smirked at me. "Where's your Easter spirit?"

"Not on the coffee table, that's for sure."

"There are four eggs, Watson. If they are not physically present, they are certainly there metaphorically."

"I dare say I can accept that," I said.

"One of the four is three inches in length. The other three are smaller, and all I will tell you of them is that they collectively equal the volume of the larger egg, that they are all precisely similar in shape to their larger cousin, and that they differ from each other in length by half an inch from short to medium, and by half an inch from medium to long."

I sighed. "I suppose you want me to puzzle out their lengths?"

"Just that of the shortest of all will do."

Can you find the answer?

✳ Solution on page 221 ✳

THREE MEN

"I came across an interesting little exercise that might benefit you, Watson. It'll test your powers of reasoning, and nothing else."

I put down my book, and grabbed a pencil and notepad. "Fire away, old chap."

"Excellent. On a theoretical train, the conductor, driver and ticket inspector are, in no particular order, named Smith, Jones and Robinson. As luck – or, in this instance, contrivance – would have it, there are also three passengers with the same surnames, whom I will refer to as Mr Smith, Mr Jones, and Mr Robinson, in order to distinguish them from that train's staff."

"Very well," I said.

"There are several pieces of information I can give you. One, Mr Robinson lives in Brixton, whilst the conductor lives in Chelsea. Two, Mr Jones cannot do algebra. Three, Smith regularly beats the ticket inspector at billiards. Four, the passenger who shares the conductor's name lives in Tottenham. Finally, five, the conductor shares his local pub with the passenger who works as a professor of mathematical physics at University College, London."

I frantically finished jotting down notes. "I have all that," I told Holmes.

"In that case, please be so good as to let me know the name of the driver. I'll warn you now that there is insufficient information to calculate every particular of every man, but there is enough to identify the driver."

Can you find the solution?

✳ Solution on page 222 ✳

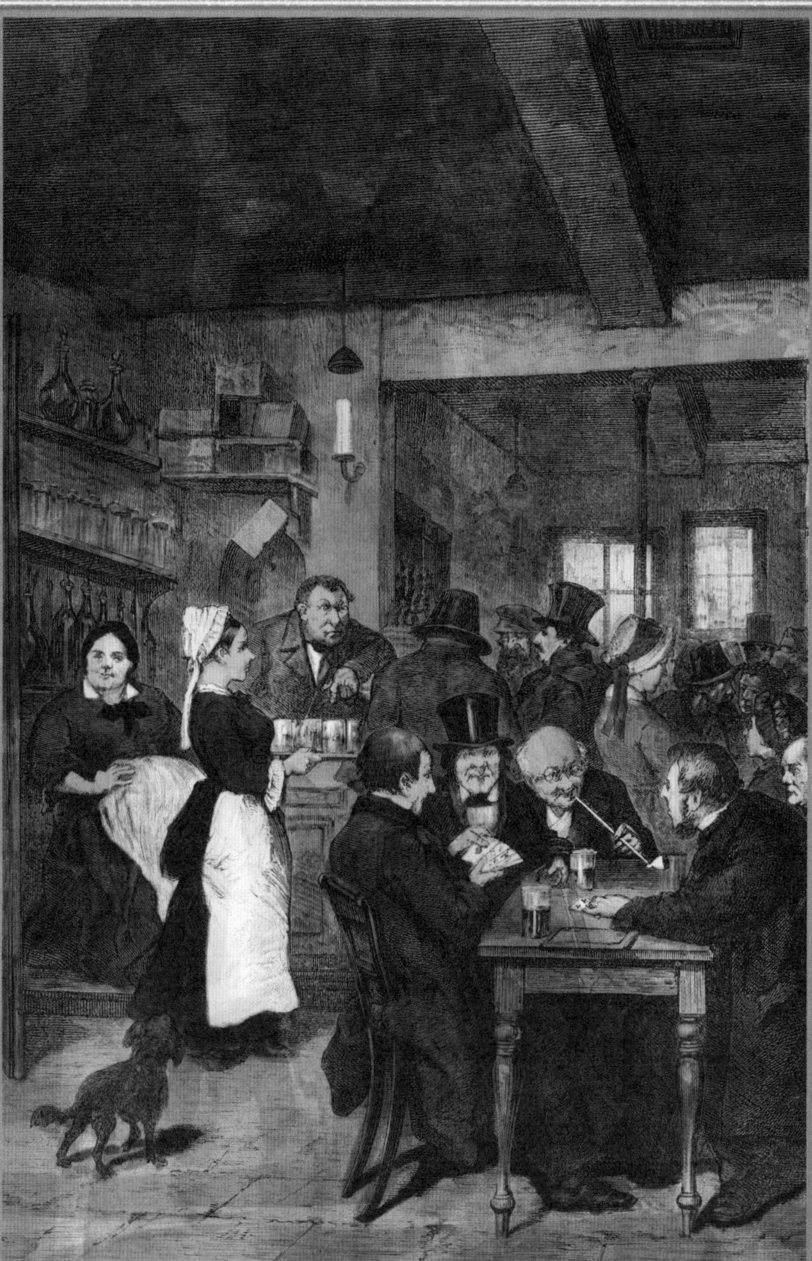

RUFUS

When Holmes and I met with Wiggins one afternoon, he was accompanied by a rather scrappy-looking mutt, who eyed me with evident suspicion.

"This is Rufus," Wiggins said. "He's a friend."

"Charmed," I said.

"He's very energetic," Wiggins told us. "Just this morning, he and I set out for a little walk."

At the word 'walk', the dog barked happily.

"When we set out, he immediately dashed off to the end of the road, then turned round and bounded back to me. He did this four times in total, in fact. After that, he settled down to match my speed, and we walked the remaining 81 feet to the end of the road at my pace. But it seems to me that if I tell you the distance from where we started to the end of the road, which is 625 feet, and that I was walking at four miles an hour, you ought to be able to work out how fast Rufus goes when he's running."

"Indeed we should," said Holmes, and turned to look at me expectantly.

What's the dog's running speed?

✳ Solution on page 222 ✳

MANUAL

I was at the table, reading my paper, when Holmes appeared from his study. "I have a little something for you, Watson," he said. "It might prove more educational than the cricket scores."

———————

"I suppose anything is possible," I said, and moved my paper.

In its place, Holmes set down three truncated cones made of paper, and ten pennies. I eyed them uncertainly.

"Do you think it possible to distribute those pennies between these makeshift paper cups so that each cup contains an odd number of pennies, with no pennies left over?"

I thought about it for a moment. "No."

He clapped me on the shoulder. "Let me know when you've succeeded."

Can you see the solution?

✳ Solution on page 223 ✳

THE TYRANT

"I should warn you, Watson, that I am a vengeful, bloody-minded tyrant."

I looked round at Holmes, and deliberately kept my face straight. "I've long suspected it," I told him.

"Which is why I'm about to have you executed," he replied. "Luckily for you, my religion permits you a get-out clause."

"That's a relief," I said.

"I will present you with two identical large jars, along with 50 white marbles, and 50 black marbles. You are to distribute these marbles between the two jars however you wish, so long as all 100 are used. One of these jars will then be chosen at random, and if you withdraw a white marble from it, your life will be spared."

"That seems oddly specific for a religion."

"It's an oddly specific religion," Holmes replied. "How would you maximize your chances of escape?"

❋ Solution on page 223 ❋

THE FINAL CAMOUFLAGE

In sharp contrast to the gentle circumstances in which Holmes assigned me his final wordknot, he waited until I was actively ill with a heavy cold before tasking me with his final word camouflage. I was feeling thoroughly sorry for myself that morning, not to mention fuzzy-headed, and I did not respond particularly well. Holmes, of course, was utterly unbothered, so in the end I worked on his puzzle anyway.

The four words that he assigned me were gatecrashed, hyperboles, subceiling and godfathered. My task was to find the small words hidden with the larger, one per word, such that the four small words were grouped together by a loose theme.

Can you discover the theme?

✳ Solution on page 223 ✳

SEVEN APPLEWOMEN

A rather odd affair, this one. It was inspired, once again, by Hookland. Holmes said that he came across it in an old book, and felt that it would serve as an unusually stringent test of my poor, battered faculties. Like many of its ilk, it is contrived to the point of utter lunacy, but even so, it may prove interesting.

* ◆ *

In a Hookland market, there are seven applewomen, who have the suspiciously regularised amounts of 20, 40, 60, 80, 100, 120, and 140 apples to sell. Being friends – and somewhat peculiar – they decide on a variable pricing scheme for their wares which will ensure that when each sells her entire consignment, each will come away with the same amount of money. Why they didn't just pool up all the takings and divide them equally is quite beyond me. Perhaps it's due to the same religious requirements that forced Holmes' theoretical tyranny to give the condemned a basket of marbles.

Still. Can you work out the pricing scheme?

❋ Solution on page 224 ❋

TERMINUS

Maxwell Perry had died in a small alley just the right side of Brick Lane, shot in the chest. His attire suggested that he'd been in something of a panic – his shoes were unlaced, his trousers belted but unbuttoned, and his jumper both back to front and inside out. Profound though his alarm had clearly been, it had just as clearly not saved him.

———◆———

As investigations unfolded, it became clear that Perry was involved in the opium trade, moving his death towards natural causes. Unfortunately, he was also a distant cousin of someone of note, and poor Inspector Lestrade was on the receiving end of a considerable amount of pressure to solve the murder. Having a whole pile of witnesses and suspects didn't help.

Holmes grudgingly agreed to have a look over Lestrade's notes, mainly to get the fellow out of our rooms. When they arrived he flicked through them, making desultory comments as he went. "Brinton claims to have seen the victim running past like 'a sack of monkeys', whatever that means... Murphy heard a shot, and found the body, but didn't see anyone else, which seems short-sighted at best... Bligh remembers seeing the victim running away because of the visible jumper label... Colgate saw one man shoot another, face to face, but was too far to get even the slightest useful detail... Routledge found a pistol in a waste skip behind a pub... Oliver says the victim turned a corner and almost barrelled into him, then shrieked and dashed off..." He dropped the file. "That's more than enough, I think. It's quite blatant who killed the man."

What did Holmes mean?

✳ Solution on page 224 ✳

ELEMENTARY ANSWERS

ON THE STRAND

The teacher and the tailor were both women, and
therefore vanishingly unlikely to be named Hugo.

GRANDDAD

As Holmes has often said, "Once you eliminate the impossible,
whatever remains, no matter how improbable, must be the
truth." The highwayman married late in life, and the grandfather
in question was her mother's father, not her father's father.

SPHERES

Three points on a sphere will always be able to be
encompassed by one hemisphere. If you visualize two points
on the boundary of one hemisphere and the third tipping
over an edge into the other, it should be immediately obvious
that all three then fall within the reverse of that first
hemisphere. Once you escape the idea that the hemispheres
are fixed in some pre-decided pattern, the matter is very
simple. Being a certainty of course, the probability is 1.

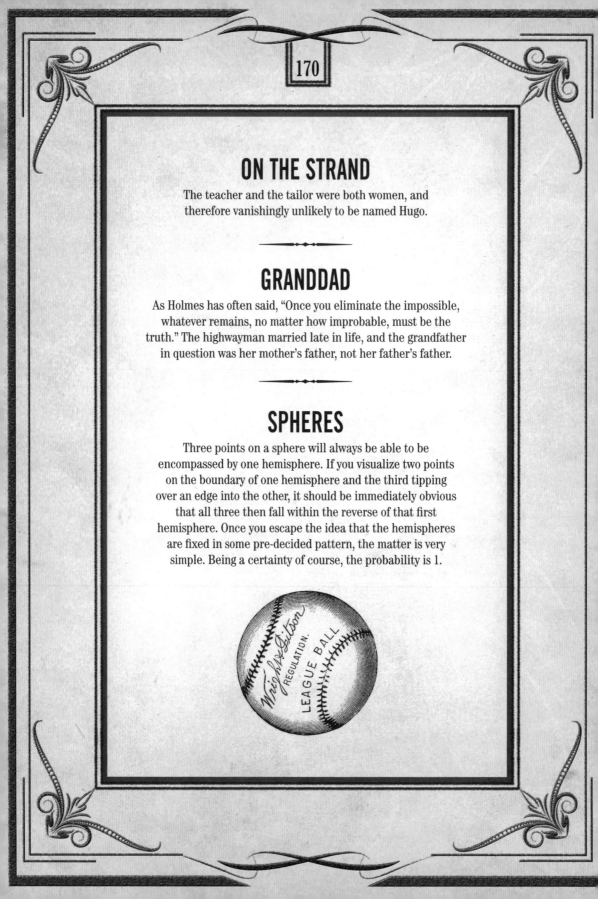

HOOKLAND

The minimum number to meet those conditions would be seven moles – 3 of them totally blind, 2 blind in the right eye, 1 blind in the left eye, and 1 with normal vision. You'll note that seven left eyes (4 blind, 3 sighted) and seven right eyes (five blind, 2 sighted) are specifically mentioned. The maximum, of course, would be fifteen, $5 + 4 + 3 + 2 + 1$.

THE WATCHMEN

As it turned out, it was rather obvious, yes. Picture the route as a circle, and imagine the guards setting off both clockwise and anti-clockwise simultaneously. There inevitably comes a moment where the two guards will meet. That is the time (and place) where the guard will have to be every hour, whichever way he is walking.

THE PRISON

Since you can make any number between 00000 and 99999, and no others, there are precisely 100,000 possible combinations for the lock.

THE FIRST WORDKNOT

The words are *chocolates*, *delicacies* and *peppermint*.

WHISKY

Seven shillings is 84p. If the whisky is worth 80 pence more than the glass, and the glass is worth x, then (80+x) is the value of the whisky, and x+80+x = 84. So the glass is worth tuppence, or 2 pence.

COUSIN TRACY

3. As both Tracy and Albert have six children, and the children of their marriage must be counted for both of them, they must have had the same number of children before they were married. There are only four possibilities, from 1 child together and 5 each separately (a total of 11) to 5 children together, and 1 each separately (a total of 7). We know the total is nine children, so both Tracy and Albert had 3 children each before marrying, and then 3 more together.

PASSING BY

The two trains running in opposite directions go 400+200=600ft (relative to each other) in 5 seconds, a total relative speed of 600/5 = 120ft/s. If running in the same direction, they would travel the same relative distance in 15 seconds, at a total speed of 600/15 = 40ft/s. So x + y = 120, and x − y = 40. As x-y=40, x=40+y, so y + 40 + y = 120, or 2y=80. Thus y = 80/2, or 40. So then x + 40 = 120, and x = 80. As 80 is greater than 40, the faster train is moving at 80ft/s – which, incidentally, is 54.54 miles per hour, as 1 f/s is approximately 0.682 mph. Do note that you'd have had to receive further information to be able to say which train was the faster (it was the shorter, if you're curious).

THE CANDLES

There are lots of numbers that are difficult to get to, but 100 can be achieved with two boxes of 16 candles, and four boxes of 17.

TRILOGY

If the former officer died without regaining consciousness, there is no way anyone could know what he had been dreaming about. The story has to be a fabrication.

BUCKETS

The weights would be identical. An object floating in water displaces an amount of water such that the weight of the water displaced is precisely equal to the weight of the object.

THE MADDENED MILLER

One ninth of a bushel. If the miller took a tenth, then 1 bushel must be 9/10ths of the flour, so the original volume would have been 1 * 10/9 bushels, or 1 and 1/9th.

THE FIRST CAMOUFLAGE

The words are *ant*, *bee*, *bug* and *moth*, and they are all types of insect.

FABULOUS

22. The arrogant runner (A) has travelled 1/6th of the course. During the time he has been running, his opponent has run 5/6ths – 1/8th of the course (because of his head-start). Convert that to 24ths, and A has gone 4/24ths while B has gone 17/24ths. We can drop the divisors to say that A runs 4 while B runs 17, so B is moving 17/4 times faster than A. A has five times as far to go, however. So to just tie with B, A would need to run at (17/4)*5 times his original speed, or 21.25 times. So to win, rounding to the nearest whole number, A would need to go 22 times as fast as he had been going.

OUT EAST

60%. The same number of men and women must have been married, so whatever number that is, it represents 2.1% of men and 1.4% of women. Simplifying those numbers, we see that the ratio of male to female inhabitants must be 2:3. So 3/5ths of the population – 60% – are female.

THE SUICIDE

There was no source of liquid anywhere in the room. Whilst not strictly impossible that our client's uncle had forced himself to dry-swallow a score of large pills, it did seem an unlikely inconvenience to inflict on oneself during one's last moments. In fact, he'd been poisoned, and although the killer staged the pills and removed the poisoned beverage, he totally forgot to replace the latter.

SCARVES

0. It's impossible. If eleven of the scarves have gone to their correct owners, then the twelfth must also have gone to its own owner too. There's no-one else for it to go to.

JOE

Joe is 10 and Ruth is 4. The only time when relative ages move so swiftly is when one of the people is very young. If you try 1 as Ruth's initial age, you'll quickly see that all the ratios pan out – 1 and 7, 2 and 8, and 3 and 9, which makes them currently 4 and 10.

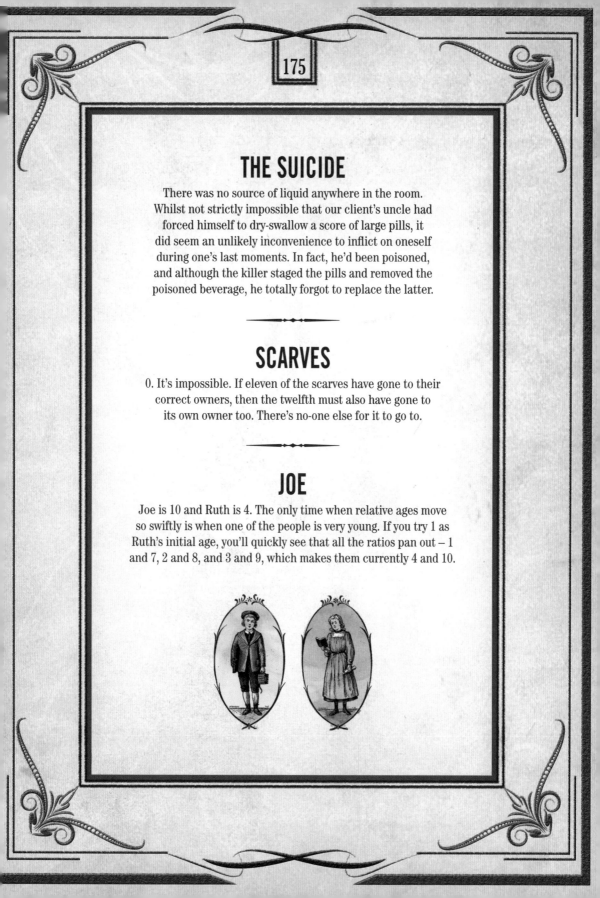

THE WENNS

33. Since there are more patrons than numbers of pennies, and no sum of pennies can be duplicated, the number of pennies each patron has must be represented by a continuous arithmetical distribution of rising 0, 1, 2, 3, etc. With both duplicate amounts and 33 pennies being forbidden, a theoretical 34th patron would have no possible number of pennies to be allocated. So the most people that there can be is if there are 33 patrons ranging from 0 to 32 pennies.

MAIDA VALE

10 miles. James is going twice as fast as Gerry, and so will catch up to him in 1 hour, at the 4 mile point. The dog is thus running at 10 miles per hour, continually, for 1 hour.

SHEEP

960. David gets 1,200 sheep, as 200 is 20% of 1000. Now, x+25% = 5x/4, so to find x, we must divide by 5/4, or multiple by 4/5, which is 0.8. As 1,200 * 0.8 = 960, Caradog gets 960 sheep.

THE SECOND WORDKNOT

The words are *tourmaline*, *aquamarine* and *rhodolites*.

THE PARTNER

£800 to Gerry, and £200 to James. If a third of the business is £1,000, then the whole business must have been worth £3,000. Of this, 60% belongs to Gerry, and 40% to James. After the deal, both James and Gerry will own 33.3% of the business, so James is losing 6.6% while Gerry is losing 26.6%. Expressing those lost percentages in thirds for simplicity will give us James's loss at 20/3, and Gerry's at 80/3. So the money should be shared between James and Gerry in the ratio 20:80. Thus James should get £200, and Gerry £800.

FRUITY

7. The pear = 1 apple + 6 plums. We know that 3 apple + 1 pear = 10 plums, so replacing the pear with 1 apple + 6 plums, we get 4 apple + 6 plums = 10 plums. That means apples and plums have the same weight. We know that the pear = 1 apple + 6 plums, so since 1 apple = 1 plum, the pear weighs 7 plums.

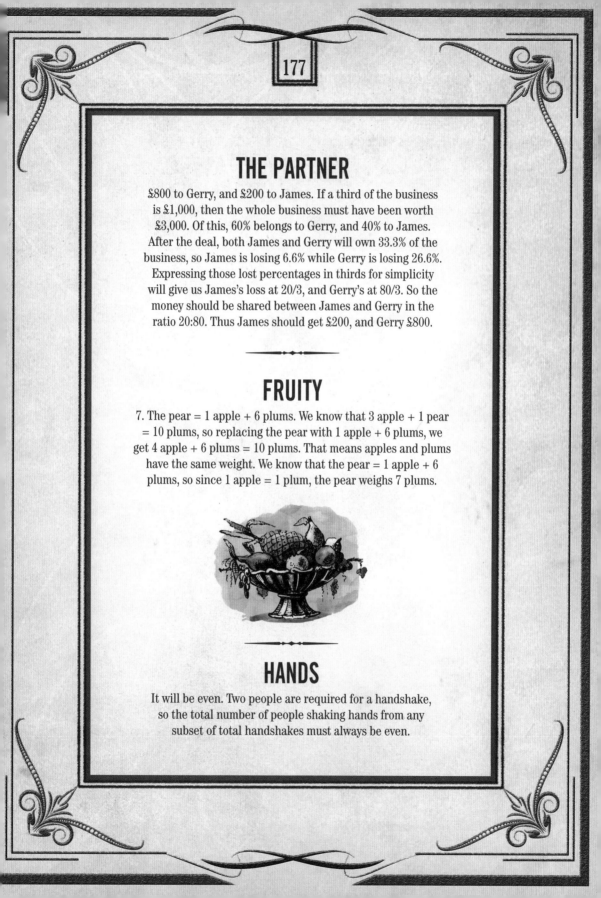

HANDS

It will be even. Two people are required for a handshake, so the total number of people shaking hands from any subset of total handshakes must always be even.

CIDER

7,890. 146+31 = 177. Dividing that into equal length and width (and remembering that one tree serves double duty at the corner) gives us a square of 89 * 89 trees. But this is the extended size of the plot, so the currently planted trees are 88 * 88 in number, or 7,744.

A SENSE OF URGENCY

Anything multiplied by 0 is 0.

HOT AND COLD

Hot air rises, so we warm things above heat sources. Cold air thus of necessity sinks. Your best option is to place the ice on top of the cube, where it can cool your metal both with physical contact, and with the cold air flowing down from the ice.

ON THE BUSES

18 miles. Smith's walking speed is a third of his riding speed, so he spends 75% of the time walking. 75% of 8 hours is 6 hours, and 6x3=18.

HOOKLAND KNIGHTS

The number 16 belongs with the second knight. On the first knight, the pairs of numbers are all made up in their entirety of curved lines. On the second knight, the pairs of numbers contain both curved and straight lines. On the third knight, the numbers are entirely made up of straight lines.

THE THIRD WORDKNOT

The words are acrobatics, daredevils, and tightropes.

THE PAINTING

The price drops to 5/8ths of its previous amount each time. I purchased it for 25/64ths of £250, which to the nearest pound is £98 – £97.65625, to be exact.

DANIEL

The corpse is on top of the rope coils. Boutros was at the bottom of the rope, and since we know he was being belayed from above, the rest of the rope was above him. Wherever the rope fell, if it had snapped – or even been let go – the rope would be next to or above the body, not beneath it. Dickey must have thrown Boutros off the top of the cliff, after one of the two of them sent the rope over (whether deliberately or accidentally).

STRAIGHTFORWARD
ANSWERS

THE PLEASANT LAKE

The missing letter is "E", and the inscription says "Persevere, ye perfect men; Ever keep these precepts ten."

THE UNCLE

He's 60. Those fractional amounts work out to 12/60ths as a child, 15/60ths as a youth and 20/60ths as a man. 12+15+20=47. 60−47=13. So 13/60ths of x, his total age = 13 years, and in turn, x=13 * 60 / 13, which is trivially 60.

SLICK

It transpires that ice is not actually slippery, no more than stone is. However, its melting point is dependent on pressure. When you put weight on it, it melts (provided that the temperature is not way below freezing), and it is the water that is slippery. It refreezes when you move on. When you walk on rough ice, you have fewer points of contact between ice and shoe, and so your weight is concentrated, increasing the pressure, the amount of water, and the slipperiness. Walking on very smooth ice spreads your weight out, and minimizes the melting.

THE SECOND CAMOUFLAGE

The words are *ear*, *eye*, *lip* and *nose*, and they are all parts of the face.

FORTY-FIVE

One of the numbers has to be a quarter of one of the others, so the larger must be divisible by 4. Together, these two must add to a little more than the sum of the other two numbers, so the largest must be a small amount less than half our target. 24 and 6 both give us 12 when operated on according to instructions, but would mean the other two had to be 14 and 10, which do not sum to 15. But 20 and 5 both give 10 when adjusted, and 45−25=20, which fits with 8 and 12. So the numbers are 8, 12, 5 and 20, and $8+2 = 12-2 = 5*2 = 20/2 = 10$.

ST MARY AXE

7.5 miles. As Lloyd spends part of the time at 5 mph and part at 3 mph, the time he spends at each speed must be in the ration 3:5. So 3 hours at 5 mph = 5 hours at 3 mph = 15 miles. But that journey would take 8 hours, not 4, so the distance is half of 15 miles.

GREAT-AUNT ADA

There are only a few pairs of digits which give a gap of 45 depending on how they're ordered. So the ages could be 05 & 50, 16 & 61, 27 & 72, 38 & 83, and 49 & 94. Of these options, the only pair of primes are 2 and 7. So Ada would be 72, making Mrs Hudson a most unlikely 27 – I can see why Holmes snorted.

RONNIE

£556. Where x is the cloak's value, x+500 = 12 (months), and x+60 = 7. Combining those, we can say that x+60 = 7*(x+500)/12. Thus 12x + 720 = 7x + 3500, so 5x = 2780, and x = 556. A modest year's salary does seem rather a staggering amount for a cape, unless it was a hand-me-down from Good Queen Bess herself, or made from overlapping scales of solid gold.

FEBRUARY

1928. There are only five of anything in February during a leap year, and then only one day, so it follows that each day of the week must get a fifth February appearance every 28 years. However, centuries are only a leap year if they are divisible by four, which rules 1900 out. The next five-Wednesday February after 1888 thus has to be 1928.

ISAAC

The trick is to obtain a pair of objects that will present an identical profile to the air, but which you can contrive to give different weight to. You then drop them, and observe them falling simultaneously. We settled on a pair of matchboxes, one with matches in and one filled with coins, but there's no end of possibilities. A pair of bottles, one empty and one full, dropped onto a cushion, perhaps.

THE CODE

Since you know the word is English, the simplest way of
finding it is a matter of discovering the one-word anagrams of
GAUNTOILER. The only one in common usage is REGULATION.
If you prefer to attack the matter mathematically, consider the
position of the numbers in the sum given. With two 5-figure
numbers adding to a 6-figure one, the first digit of the answer, R,
can only be "1". For the start of the 5-digit numbers, we see that
G+O leave G in the units again. If either G or O was 0, the answer
would be 5-digit not 6, so there must be 1 carrying over from the
next column along, and O must be '9'. Similarly, A+I >= 10, in
order to give the number to carry over. At the end, we see T+R=I,
but R is 1, so we know I must be one greater than T. N+E=E
means N must be 0. U+L must equal 9. I don't have the room
here, but keep pressing the matter on this basis, and the puzzle
will fall. The sum, incidentally, is 36,407 + 98,521 = 134,928.

THE TRACK

9 minutes 20 seconds. Blue is moving 4/7 the speed of red,
and red needs to have run blue's distance plus one whole
lap in order to pass him. After one lap of red's, blue is 3/7 of
a lap behind. After two, he's 6/7 down. It should be obvious
that red is closing the distance at exactly 3/7ths of a lap for
each lap of his own. He has 1/7th to go, so that will take him
a third of a lap. So the total distance is 2 and 1/3rd laps,
which at 4 minutes a lap is 9 minutes and 20 seconds.

A CHELSEA TALE

It turned out that Jez (short for Jeremy, apparently) is a window-cleaner. He was on the outside of the building, and when he panicked, he jumped into the room in front of him.

EXPRESS

Although I was right about the impending question, it proved not to be algebraic so much as logical. If the trains are running at 60 mph and 40 mph, then an hour ago, they were 60+40 = 100 miles apart.

THE FENCE

If the length of the fence is y feet, and the number of posts is x, then x + 150 = y = 3(x − 70) = 3x − 210. So we can say that 2x = 360, or x = 180 (and, by the by, y = which would give an area of around 6,806 sq ft if made into a square enclosure, or, maximally, an area of 8,666 sq ft as a circular area of radius 52.52ft).

THE FOURTH WORDKNOT

The words are *underscore*, *subheading* and *typesetter*.

THE ONE

It is comprised of all ten digits in English alphabetical order.

THE BISCUITS

It was Stephen. Only one of the statements is true. Since Will and Stephen's statements are mutually exclusive, the true statement must be one of them. Now, assume Stephen's statement is true, and he is innocent. In this instance, the opposites of the other statements do not give a definite solution – it could still be either Mary or Gwen, neither of whom are wrongfully accused (and thus given an alibi when their accusations are negated). Since Wiggins had an immediate solution, the statements must give a firm answer. Thus Will is telling the truth, and Stephen stole (and ate) the biscuits.

DANGEROUS LADIES

30AD. Since the ladies had a total lifespan of 69 years over the course of 129 years, there must have been sixty years when neither were alive. So Boadicea was born 60 years after 30BC – in 30AD.

SQUARE SHEEP

12. What I finally remembered is that a circle is the most perfectly compact expression of any given area, so it follows that for any given perimeter length – ie, number of matches – the closer your shape gets to a circle, the bigger the area it contains. In this instance, a perfectly regular 12-sided shape (a dodecagon) with sides of length 1 will give you an area of 11.19y2, since the area of a dodecagon is 0.5 * 12 * side-length * distance from centre to the middle of any side (which is 1.865 * side-length). Similarly, a perfectly regular 11-sided shape (an endecagon) with sides of length 1 works out at 9.365y2. So you can make a 10y2 space with 12 yard-long fences.

MR ANDREAS

£14,315. To calculate simple compound interest of this sort (that is, where the interest is calculated once per designated time unit), you can calculate the 55% manually, add it to the base sum, and repeat a series of times. But it is simpler and more efficient to use the formula $A = P * (1+r)^t$, where A is the accrued wealth, P is the principal (or initial) capital, r is the rate of interest as a fraction, and t is the number of iterations. So in this instance, $A = 1600 * (1+0.55)^5$, or 1600 * 8.9466.

THE BOTTLE

You need three measurements. First of all, measure the diameter of the base, and use that to find the area of the base. Then stand the bottle upright, and measure the height of the liquid from the base. Finally, turn the bottle upside down, and measure the height of the empty space from the top of the liquid (which will be well above the start of the neck) to the base. You now have measurements for the volume filled by liquid – the area of the base * the height of the liquid – and the volume filled by air, area of base * height of air. As there is nothing else in there, add these two together to find the volume of the bottle.

DAVEY

The only possible answer is that when Wiggins turned around and started walking towards Davey, Davey started walking backwards at the same pace. Peculiar behaviour, to be sure.

THE WATCH

Jim worked 00:00 – 06:00 and 10:00 – 16:00.

Dave worked 04:00 – 10:00 and 16:00 – 22:00.

Peter worked 12:00 – 18:00 and 22:00 – 04:00.

Mike worked 06:00 – 12:00 and 18:00 – 00:00.

THE FIFTH WORDKNOT

Twittering. Chattiness. Volubility.

THE LEASE

45. From Archie's statement, $4x/5 = 2y/3$, and $x+y = 99$. So $12x=10y$, or $x=10y/12$. Now substitute, so $10y/12+y = 99$, or $10y + 12y = 1188$, or $22y=1188$, so $y=54$. Then, $x+54 = 99$, or $x=45$. There are 45 years left.

TEA

9. First, place the 5lb and 9lb weights in different pans, so that 4lb of tea will balance them. Weigh four such 4lb lots, leaving (of necessity) 4lbs in the bale. Then take each 4lb lot in turn, remove the weights from the scales, and divide each lot so that it is perfectly balanced. This will add five weighings to the four previous, for a total of nine.

LOOSE CHANGE.

I started out with 220p, which is of course just tuppence short of nineteen shillings. The trick is to start at the end and work backwards. So $6+9+6 = 21*2 = 42 + 10 = 52*2 = 104 + 6 = 110*2 = 220$.

HOW MANY COWS

121,393. The Fibonacci sequence is a famous mathematical model describing exponential growth of precisely this kind, such that each number in the sequence is the sum of the two numbers preceding it. It runs 0, 1, 1, 2, 3, 5, 8, ..., where in this instance, the terms of the sequence would indicate the number of calves produced in that year. It is useful here to note that the sum total of all numbers up to any Nth term in the sequence is equal to the (N+2)th term minus one. Further more, as N = (N–1) + (N–2) – the basic definition of the sequence – then also (N+2) = 2*(N) + (N–1). So from those two, it follows that if we know two sequential terms, N and N–1, then the total of all the values in the sequence up to N is equal to 2*(N) + (N–1) –1. The 24th and 25th terms of the sequence are 48,368 and 28,657, so the black woodland cow would have a total of 2*(48,368)+(28,657)–1=121,392 descendants in that time. She, of course, is still active, for a total 121,393 cows. That's a lot of cows behaving quite oddly, so I can see Mr Podge's concern somewhat.

ODD

My eventual answer was to combine two 1s to make 11, so that 11 + 1 + 1 + 1 = 14. You could do it other ways if you added in other mathematical operations – 1/1 + 9 + 3 + 1, for example.

DRAFT

As the window cools, the air in the room next to it gets colder. Cold air sinks, so the warmer air of the room gets pulled down to fill the space. Then it too chills. This effect produces a circular draft from fireplace to window, with warm air running along the ceiling, and cold air along the floor. We feel this as a draft. This is part of the reason why Mr San Galli's excellent heating radiators are often placed below windows.

THE SEAMSTRESS

When it's dark, it's very hard to see anything outside from a lit room. This is particularly true when it's raining, no matter how lightly. Since the house is in a rural environment, there would have been nothing in the way of extra light to illuminate the fellow. She must have made up the intruder to prepare the way for some other mischief to take place.

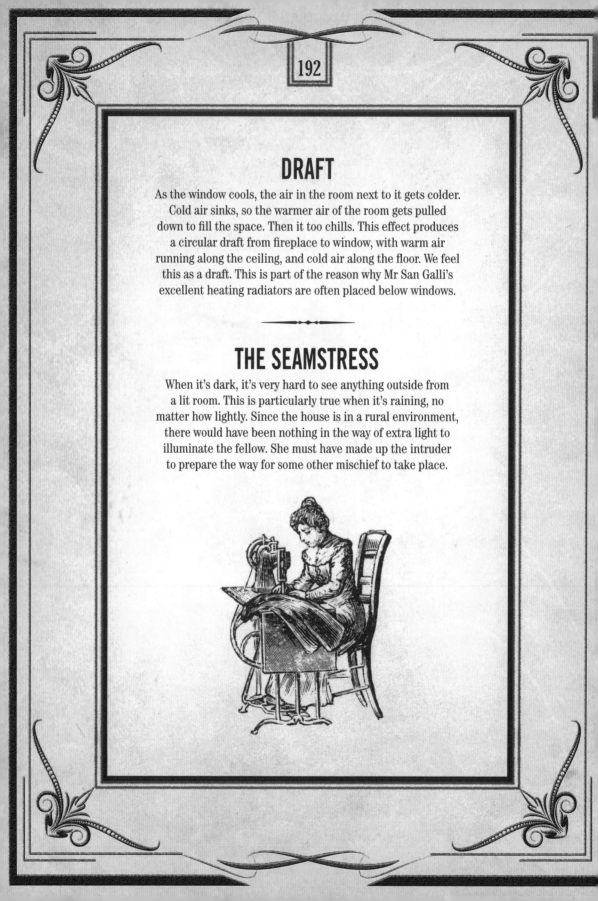

BEES

Just 15 bees, which seems to me to be a low estimate by a factor of 1,000, even for a small hive. Still, we must tackle the situation as expressed by Holmes's correspondent. We know that two of the factions of bees represent 1/5th and 1/3rd of the workers. Expressing those figures in a common denominator makes for 3/15ths and 5/15ths. The difference between these amounts is 2/15ths, which multiplied by 3 gives us 6/15ths. These bees account for 3+5+6=14/15ths of the workers. The remaining 1/15th of the workers is 1 bee, so 1*15 = 15.

FRUITFUL

It is just three pieces of fruit, one of each type, as a moment's thought will swiftly make clear.

THE THIRD CAMOUFLAGE

The words were *bill*, *fund*, *loss* and *sell*, and the theme was business.

SPEED

Sid won again. In the previous races, Ray ran 90y whilst Sid ran 100y. So in the last race, Ray and Sid would be neck and neck at the 90-yard point, Ray having run 90y and Sid 100y. In the remaining 10y, Sid continued outpacing Ray and won.

CUNNING ANSWERS

THE WEIGHTS

30lb. The three together weight 180, and man and child
are 162lb more than the dog, so the dog weighs half
the difference between 162 and 180. 180–162=18/2=9.
The dog is 30 per cent of the child's weight. 9/30*100
= 30, giving us the weight of the baby.

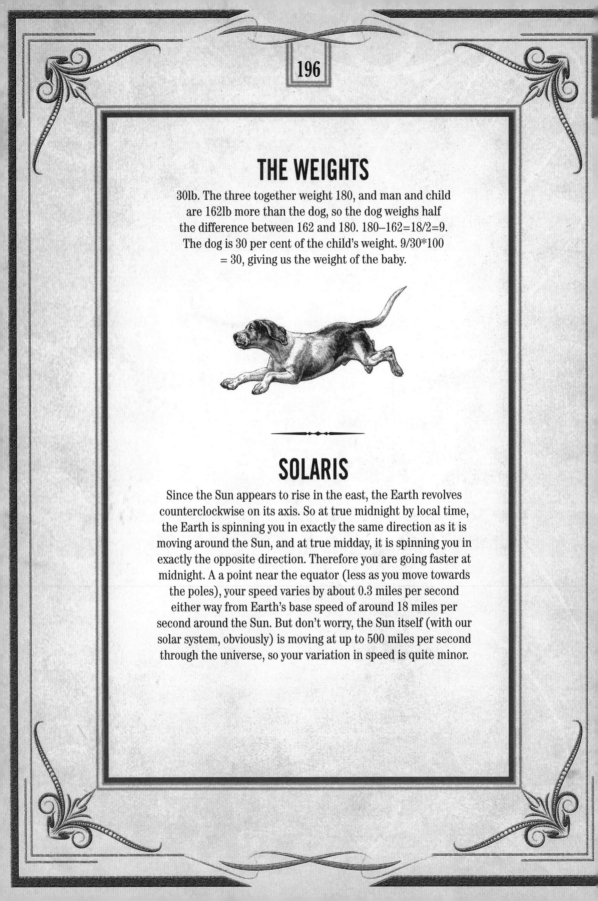

SOLARIS

Since the Sun appears to rise in the east, the Earth revolves
counterclockwise on its axis. So at true midnight by local time,
the Earth is spinning you in exactly the same direction as it is
moving around the Sun, and at true midday, it is spinning you in
exactly the opposite direction. Therefore you are going faster at
midnight. A a point near the equator (less as you move towards
the poles), your speed varies by about 0.3 miles per second
either way from Earth's base speed of around 18 miles per
second around the Sun. But don't worry, the Sun itself (with our
solar system, obviously) is moving at up to 500 miles per second
through the universe, so your variation in speed is quite minor.

A WORSHIP OF WRITERS

Tomkins. From the information given, Squires must the playwright, Appleby the historian, Whitely the humorist, Archer the poet, Gardner the short story writer, and Tomkins the novelist.

LOGGERS

360ft cubic feet of wood, which works out at a little over 2.8 cords. The relative amount of time Doug and Dave spend sawing and splitting must match the ratio of how much of each job they can perform in one day – that is, they must divide their day by 6:9, or 2:3. Thus they must spend 3/5ths of the day sawing, which is slower, and 2/5ths of the day splitting. 3/5ths of 600 is 360 cubic feet of wood (as is 2/5ths of 900).

THE SIXTH WORDKNOT

The words were violinists, trumpeters, and pianoforte.

TWO SUMS

The first answer is 12+78 = 34+56 (=90). Bearing in mind that larger and smaller numbers will average towards median numbers will help this discovery. The second is 173+4 = 85+92 = 177, and if there is a way to find the answer without trial and error, I do not know it.

DUCK DUCK GOOSE

4 shillings. Starting with 1 for a chicken gives you 2 for a duck, which, in the second equation of $3c + d = 2g$ would mean that $3*1 + 1*2 = 2*goose = 5$. But we can't have 2.5 shillings for a goose. So double the chicken and duck prices. $3*2 + 1*4 = 10$, giving 5 for a goose. Try that in the third equation of $3g + 1c + 2d = 25$. $3*5 + 1*2 + 2*4 = 15 + 2 + 8 = 25$. So 5s, 4s and 2s are the correct prices, and a duck is 4s.

THE JEWELLER

75 minutes. If going to and from work by cab takes 30 minutes, one way takes 15 minutes. The walking part of the journey with a return cab must be 15 minutes less than the combined time. 90–15=75 minutes.

THE NOTE

13 21 13 21 32 21 12. Speak the digits aloud, and it will become clear that each line is described by the numbers in the following line – so "One 2"; then "One one, one two"; then "Three 1s, one 2," and so on.

SERPENTINE

The level of the water will fall slightly. If Sieger sinks, he must be denser than water on average. When an item floats, it displaces water equal to its weight, but when submerged, displaces water equal to its volume. Since he sinks, he's heavier than the amount of water his volume would weigh, and suddenly takes up less displaced water, lowering the water level.

THE LEGACY

£24. We know that x + y = 100, and that x/4 − y/3 = 11. Multiply out the divisors in that second equation (i.e. *12), and you get 3x − 4y = 132. Now x=100−y, so 3*(100−y) − 4y = 132, and 300 − 3y − 4y = 132, or 7y = 300 − 132 = 168. So y = 168/7 = 24. (And x, Frederick's bequest, must be £76).

CHILDREN

3 of one and 1 of the other is more likely. There are 16 possibilities (2 options, 4 times = 2^4 = 16), all equally likely. Of those, 2 are single-gender, BBBB and GGGG. Eight are 3–and–1: BGGG, GBGG, GGBG, GGGB, and their opposites. Six are two of each – BBGG, BGBG, BGGB, and their opposites. So there's a 8/16 (or 50%) chance of three children of one gender, a 6/16 (or 37.5%) chance of two of each gender, and a 2/16 (or 12.5%) chance of all the children being the same gender. As an aside, do note that about 1 human pregnancy in 90 produces twins, which may somewhat complicate a more precise calculation, and in practice, the chance of a male birth is very rarely exactly 50%, so the terms of this question are not rigorous reflections of reality.

THE REVENGE

Blaydon refers to the Revenge as "it", not "she", in direct contravention of all English-speaking naval tradition.

THE TRUNK

35 yards. We don't know the tractor's speed, but it moves a certain distance – Y – for each pace Holmes takes. So when he has moved 140 yards, the front of the tree has moved 140Y yards. Holmes has walked that distance plus the length of the tree, x, in that time, so in yards, 140 = x +140Y. In the other direction, Holmes has walked 20 paces, so the tip of the tree has moved 20Y yards. Since they're going in opposite directions, their combined distance equals the length of the tree, and x = 20 + 20Y. So now we have x = 20 + 20Y, and x = 140 – 140Y. So 20 + 20Y = 140 – 140Y, and 1+Y = 7–7Y, thus 8Y=6, or Y=0.75. Since x=20+20Y, then x=20+15 = 35 yards.

THE FIELD

40 days. Let us measure in a unit of "fields per day", so we then have C + G = 1/45, C + L = 1/60, and G + L = 1/90. Our first task is to compare like with like. The lowest common denominator of those fractions is 1/360th. So 1C + 1G + 0L = 8/360, 1C+ 0G + 1L = 6/360, and 0C + 1G + 1L = 4/360. Substituting the first equation (ordered to solve for C) C = (8/360 – 1G), into the second, so (8/360 – 1G) +1L = 6/360, and 2/360 +1L = 1G. Substitute this into the third, 2/360 + 1L + 1L = 4/360, or L = 1/360. Track back to the second now to solve for G, and 2+360 + 1/360 = G = 3/360, and finally back once more for C = 8/360 – 3/360 = 5/360. So the lamb eats 1/360th of a field a day, the goat 3/360ths, and the cow 5/360ths. Since they're all in there together, they get through 1+3+5=9/360ths of a field a day. 360/9 = 40, so they'll eat all the grass in 40 days.

THE TYPE

27. In order to be able to form each month in full, you need the following twenty-seven letters – AA, B, C, D, EEE, F, G, H, I, J, L, M, N, OO, P, RR, S, T, UU, V, and Y.

STABBING

The butler. He claims to have tripped over the body in the darkness, and yet to have seen the victim lying on the floor from outside the room. He's clearly lying.

BALANCE

No matter how a coin is weighted, if you flip it twice, it will always generate a head immediately followed by a tails precisely as often as it generates a tails immediately followed by a head. So throw the coin twice. Then HT is one fair possibility, and TH is the other. If you get any other result, throw the coin twice more. On the most blatantly weighted coins, you might require some patience, but the toss will remain fair. Obviously you'll be waiting a very, very long time if the coin has two identical faces.

THE MANAGER

36. Go back x years, and the deputy was half the manager's current age, making him 24, and the manager the deputy's current age, y. So y − x = 24, and because the difference between ages will stay constant, y + x = 48. Thus 2y = 72, and the deputy is 36.

GETTING AHEAD

It took me a while, and a little prompting, but eventually I hit on volumetric comparison by submersion in water. For example, you could fill a bucket with water, and place it inside am empty tub. Submerge the waxed head in the bucket, and water equal to its volume will spill into the tub. Pour this run-off into one of several similar glass jars. You can then re-fill the bucket, and submerge the vegetable into the bucket, again gathering the over-spill. Compare the run-offs, and you'll be able to see which is closest to the original. I have never come across this story in any other source, so for now, please consider it whimsy rather than historical truth.

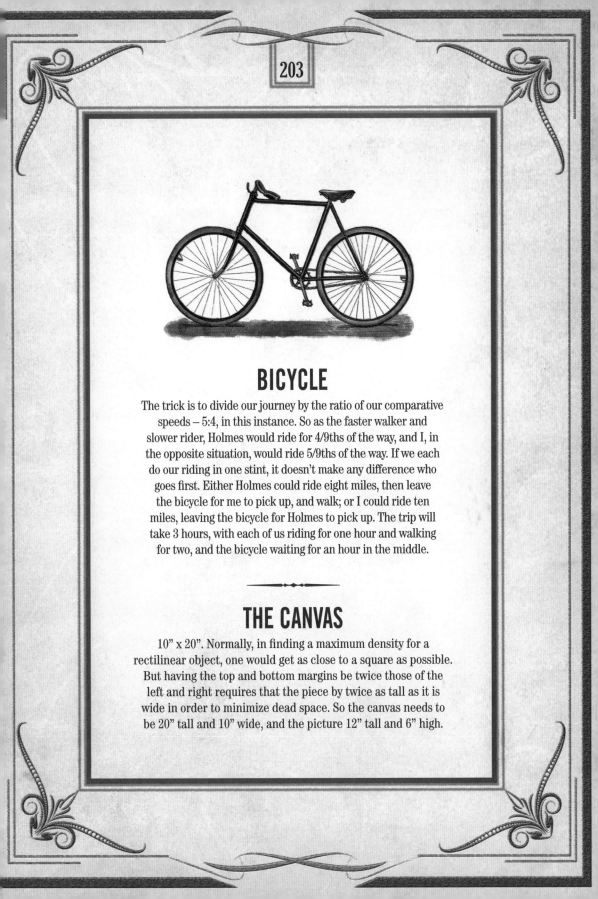

BICYCLE

The trick is to divide our journey by the ratio of our comparative speeds – 5:4, in this instance. So as the faster walker and slower rider, Holmes would ride for 4/9ths of the way, and I, in the opposite situation, would ride 5/9ths of the way. If we each do our riding in one stint, it doesn't make any difference who goes first. Either Holmes could ride eight miles, then leave the bicycle for me to pick up, and walk; or I could ride ten miles, leaving the bicycle for Holmes to pick up. The trip will take 3 hours, with each of us riding for one hour and walking for two, and the bicycle waiting for an hour in the middle.

THE CANVAS

10" x 20". Normally, in finding a maximum density for a rectilinear object, one would get as close to a square as possible. But having the top and bottom margins be twice those of the left and right requires that the piece by twice as tall as it is wide in order to minimize dead space. So the canvas needs to be 20" tall and 10" wide, and the picture 12" tall and 6" high.

PIG

15. Either you found this easy, or you need to hold on to your hats, my friends. It is genuinely straight forward, but it requires several steps. We know that $95x + 97y = 4238$, and that the numbers of both pigs and sheep must be non-zero integers. Indeterminate equation theory allows a solution. First, solve our equation for x, where $x = (4238/95) - (97y/95)$, and reduce the right-hand side into integers and fractions as far as possible: $x = 44 + 58/95 - y - 2y/95$, which simplifies to $x = 44 - y + (58-2y)/95$. Now, since x is an integer, the right-hand term also must be an integer. As 44 and y are both integers as well, that last bit $(58-2y)/95$ must also be an integer, albeit one we are utterly unsure of. Let's call that value "2i" just for now. We can then rearrange our new definition of $2i = (58-2y)/95$ in terms of y as $y = 29 - 95i$. But y is an non-negative integer, so $0 <= 29 - 95i$, and $i <= 29/95$. We now have a term for y that we can substitute back in the equation for x, so $x = 44 - (29 - 95i) + (58 - 2*(29 - 95i))95$, and although that looks ugly, a lot of it cancels out, and it simplifies down to $x = 44 - 29 + 95i + 2i$, or $x = 15 + 97i$. Again, x must be an integer, so $0 <= 15 + 97i$, and $-15/97 <= i$. So now we have a range where $-15/97 <= i <= 29/95$, and since i also has to be an integer, in this case it must be 0. Finally, we have equations for both x and y expressed in terms of i, so $x = 15 + 97*0$, or 15, and $y = 29 - 95*0$, or 29. Pigs were x, so he bought 15 pigs. You can approach any indeterminate equation using this method, although equations with more unknowns require commensurately more steps. If the equation is insoluble, your range for i will be impossible.

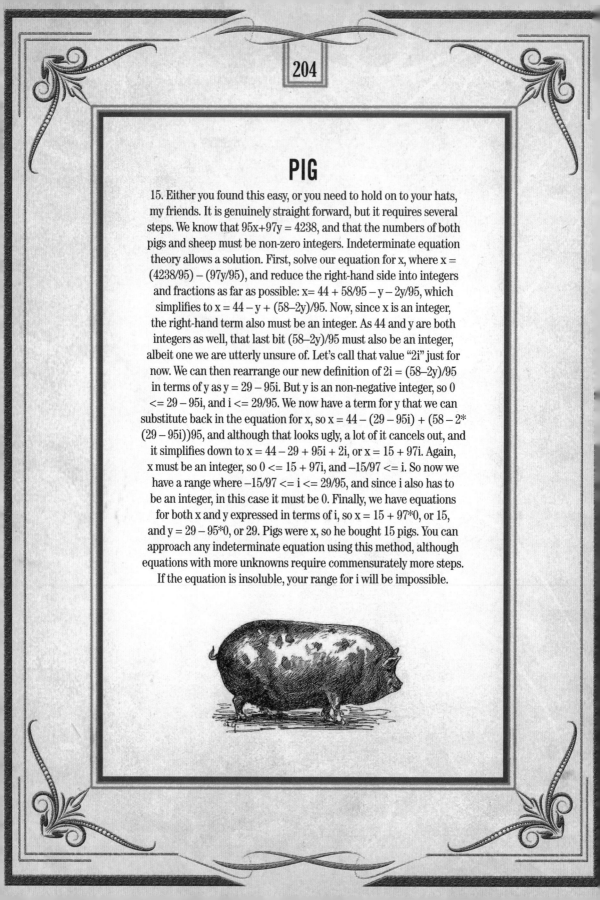

THE SEVENTH WORDKNOT

The three words were *picaresque*, *dishonesty* and
mountebank, and the theme was roguery.

THE SHOPKEEPER

Digits to make up a larger number. In this instance,
they were brass, and clearly intended to screw into
a front door to display the house number.

MATCH TWO

Take ten matches, and use them to spell out the word
FIVE. Then remove seven of the ten matches, leaving
just the letters IV, "4" in Roman numerals. Simple
when you know how – but then, most puzzles are.

CURIO

3&5, and 7&8. To solve this mathematically, we need to address a little more indeterminacy. We know that $x^2 + x*y + y^2 = a$ square number. We can use $(x-a*y)^2$ to represent the square number, as this will always be squared, and the variable term 'a' allows us to come to any square for a given x,y. We can then expand this square term from $(x-ay)*(x-ay)$ to $x^2 - 2axy + (a^2)(y^2)$. From that, we can see that $x+y = ya^2 - 2ax$. Add $(-y+2ax)$ to each side again, and it will simplify down to $x+2ax = ya^2-y$, and $x(2a+1)=y(a^2-1)$. Therefore, as the terms have to balance out to $xy=yx$, then $x=a^2-1$, and $y=2a+1$. When $a=1$, this gives us 0,2 for x,y – which works, but we need numbers from 1–9. So $a=2$ gives 3,5, and $a=3$ gives 8,7. Note than $a=4$ gives $x>9$. Personally, I stuck to the brute force solution.

SIX FEET UNDER

Ten feet below the surface, the seasonal temperatures in the temperate zone are up to four months behind air temperature. If it was the end of spring on the surface, it would still have been winter for the moles and earthworms. Below 75 feet or so, there is almost no seasonal variation at all – at least, here in London.

ENGINE TROUBLE

200 miles. Say x is the distance from the spot where the engine fault developed to the destination, and y is full speed. We then know that the normal time "t" to complete the journey is t=x/y, that at 3/5ths of y, the time is t+2 = 5x/3y, and that if we'd gone 50 miles further we'd have arrived 1 hour 20 minutes late, so t+4/3 = 50/y + 5(x–50)/3y. Substitute t=x/y through the second equation, and you'll quickly find that t has to be 3, and x=3y. So we would normally have had 3 hours left to go, making a typical four-hour journey, and the distance left would have had to be 3 times the normal top speed in miles per hour. Now we know the third equation gets us there 2/3 of an hour sooner than the second, so substitute t+2 = 5x/3y into the third equation, and 5x/3y – 2/3 = 50/y + 5x/3y – 250/3y, so 5x – 2y = 150 + 5x – 50, and 2y = 100. Thus full speed is 50mph and, finally, our full distance takes four hours at 50 mph to travel, so must be 200 miles.

RECALL

28. Start at the back and work forwards, reversing the operations as you go, and it is easy. 2*10 = 20, –8 = 12, *12 = 144, +52 = 196, sq rt = 14, * 3/2 = 21, * 7 = 147, * 4/7 = 84, / 3 = 28. Note that *4/7 reverses +75% because 4/4 + 3/4 = 7/4.

MORAN

Yes, actually. You need to remember that the first shot marks the start of the time count, and so counts as $t=0$, not $t=5s$. To meet his boast precisely, the gun would have had to shoot 60 rounds in 4 minutes and 55 seconds. The same principle is why if you put two points on a piece of paper, one line segment connects them rather than two.

THE EIGHTH WORDKNOT

The words are *hoodwinked*, *handcuffed* and *restrained*.

BARNABAS

2 half-crowns. We know the work-rate of both people is consistent between the two tasks. Wiggins can shovel as quickly as Barnabas can dig, but he can dig four times faster than Barnabas can shovel. There are two steps required in comparing Wiggins digging to Barnabas digging, but as the work-rate is same in both steps, Wiggins' work rate is 2 to Barnabas' 1. So however they broke down the jobs, and however long it took, Wiggins was twice as good a worker as Barnabas, and the money should be split 2:1.

THE FORTY-FOUR

20 and 64. You could use trial and error to find two plausible ages 44 years apart that multiply to 1280, but there is also an algebraic solution. We have x*y=1280 and x–y=44. So x=44+y. This gives us 44y+y^2 = 1280, or reordering into a standard quadratic, y^2 + 44y – 1280 = 0. From the quadratic formula, y = (–b +– sq root (b^2 – 4ac))/2a, where a, b and c are the multiples of each term in order. Note that +– means you have to solve twice, once adding the square root, and once subtracting it. In our case, a is 1 (for just y^2), b is 44, and c = –1280. So we have (–44 +– sq rt (44^2 – (4*1*–1280))) / 2, which once you sort out the arithmetic, breaks down to (–44 +– 84) / 2 = –64 and +20. We're just looking for magnitudes for the ages (the single minus arrives since we were given the difference between the two ages, not the sum), so Michael is 64 and Minnie is 20.

THE MURDER OF MOLLY GLASS

Mrs Glass had lit the fire in her bedroom before going to sleep. Once she was slumbering, her husband turned off the gas line to the house. The fire duly went out. Then he switched the gas back on again, so that it built up unhindered in her bedroom, and asphyxiated her.

FIENDISH ANSWERS

PIPE DREAMS

Definitely not in one generation, no. Roughly half of pregnancies produce boys, so initially, half of the mothers would stop producing children. Of those that remained, again roughly half would produce boys, and stop. This pattern would continue indefinitely. At each stage, the expectant mothers remaining would produce as many boys as girls, so the gender balance would not change, but the number of children would plummet, and the population contract. It is not impossible that some women might have a genetic predisposition to produce more girls that boys, and this genetic trait would become highly selected for, but it takes an average of 75 generations or more for a mutation to spread through the population. Even a strongly selected pressure like this would still require hundreds of years to have a noticeable effect.

THE OLD ONES

The murderer was in the process of robbing the pub, and shot the victim to eliminate him as a witness. In fact, he had already murdered the landlord and the cook, at which point one more body would hardly matter. The fellow was eventually apprehended at Portsmouth docks, and duly hung.

RIFLE ROUNDS

97. Between boxes of 15 and 20, you can make any multiple of 5, so long as that is not 5, 10, or 25. So the general technique to solve any request is, if the number is not already a multiple of 5, provide boxes of 18 until you are left with a multiple of 5, and then assemble the remainder from the other boxes. The last time where this technique falls down is the number 97, where subsequent boxes of 18 leave 79, 61, 43, and finally 25. Once you get any higher, up to 5 boxes of 18 will always be enough to bring you to a multiple of 5 that you can fill. Quite ingenious.

THE PLEASANT WAY

18 miles. As a general rule for this sort of problem, triple the distance of the first meeting place, and subtract the distance of the second meeting place. So 10*3 – 12 = 18.

FASHION

20 dresses. If there are x dresses costing y each, then x*y=1800. Furthermore, we also know that (x+30)*(y–3)=1800. Since y=1800/x, then (x+30)*(1800/x – 3)=1800, and 1800/(x+30) + 3 = 1800/x. Thus 3*(x+30)x + 1800x = 1800(x+30), and 3x^2 +90x –54000 = 0. We've discussed solving quadratic equations earlier; the solution to this gives you a positive quadratic root of x=120. There were 120 dresses, each costing an eye-watering £15, of which 20 had been stolen.

THE FOURTH CAMOUFLAGE

The words are *cut*, *dig*, *sow* and *trim*, and their unifying theme
is gardening (or, more generally, agriculture, I suppose.)

THE APPLE MARKET

The truth is that the two sales methods are only directly
equivalent when the number of apples sold at three a penny is in
the proportion of 3:2 with the apples sold at two a penny. However,
that is not the case here; the proportion is 1:1. If the first woman
had had 36 apples, and the second 24, then they would have been
due 12 pence each, whether they'd sold them themselves or via
the friend. In this case, the three-a-penny lady would have earned
10 pence from her apples, and her friend
15 pence, so by splitting the money into two lots of 12 pence, the
first woman gets 2p extra, and the second woman 3 pence less.
9.5 pence and 14.5 pence would have been a fairer division.

A PAIR OF FOURS

In the end, it took me a lot of time, not a little. However, I did find
the solution – sq rt (sq rt (sq rt 4) ^ 4!). 4! is 1*2*3*4, or 24, and
sq rt 4 is obviously 2, so the equation becomes sq rt (sq rt 2)^24,
and you can write sq rt as ^0.5. Roots and powers of this sort
cancel out, so it becomes 2^0.5^0.5^24 = 2^0.5^12 = 2^6 = 64.

ASHCOURT STATION

9 (or possibly 11). As we set off, there were four Waterloo-to-Ashcourt trains en route, one just leaving Waterloo, and one in Ashcourt station. Over the next five hours, four more would depart Waterloo, with a fifth about to depart as we pulled in. Over the course of our journey, we must inevitably pass all of those trains, as there is nowhere else for them to go but past us Now to my mind, the train in Ashcourt as we departed and the train leaving Waterloo as we arrived don't really count as being "on the way", so I make the tally to be nine. If you decided you did count them, then eleven is a reasonable answer as well.

ANDREW

Just before leaving for David's house, Andrew would set the clock to twelve, and start it. When he arrived at David's, he'd note the correct time from David's clock, and he'd do the same when he left to return home, so he knew how long he'd spent with David. Then when he arrived home, he'd have a record of precisely how long he'd been away in total. Subtracting the time he'd spent at David's from this would tell him how long his journey there and back had been. Adding one half of this amount to the time when he left David's house then gave him the correct time now.

CENTURIAL

53 years and 4 months. It should be plain that if the youngest son is aged x, then $x + 2x + 4x + 8x = 100$, so $15x=100$, and $x = 6$ and 2/3rds years. Jack is 8x years old, so he's 53 and 1/3rd years old (and his sons are 26 and 2/3rds, 13 and 1/3rd, and 6 and 2/3rds.)

ROCK PAPER SCISSORS

Wiggins won, 7–3. Since there were no draws, Wiggins's 6 scissors met Alice's 4 paper and 2 rock, giving Wiggins 4 out of 6. The other games must have been Alice's scissors, which met Wiggins' rock three times, and paper once, giving Wiggins 3 out of 4. So he won 7 out of 10.

OLD HOOK

10 and 5/41sts hours. If Ted rides for x miles at 8 mph, then his journey time = (x/8) + (40–x)/1. Hob walks for y miles, so his journey time is y/2 + (40–y)/8. This means that Ern's journey time is x/8 + (x–y)/8 + (40–y)/8. Now all these total times are equal. So (x/8) + 40 – x = y/2 + (40–y)/8, which means 7x + 3y = 280. Also, by multiplying the second and third equation by 8, 4y + 40 – y = x + x – y + 40 – y, and 2x – 5y = 0. So now we have two simple equations for x and y. Solve, and we'll find that x=1400/41, and y=560/41. Note that leaving it in terms of 1/41 is simplest for this solution. Substitute x into Ted's time or y into Hob's time, and you'll find that the total is 10 and 5/41 hours.

ART

He lost £10 over all. £75 at 25% profit means that painting cost £60 originally. £75 at 25% loss means that the other painting cost £100. So he paid £160 for paintings that fetched in £150.

DAISY

The probability is 2/3, or roughly 67%. With two children, there are four possibilities, boy-boy, boy-girl, girl-boy, and girl-girl. We know only that girl-girl is impossible. So there are three options, and in two of them, one of the children is a girl.

THE NINTH WORDKNOT

The words were *trebuchets*, *musketeers* and *broadswords*.

THE SEVEN

1 in 7, or about 14%. It turns out that the total number of ways the children could sit is 5,040, or 7!, which is 7*6*5*4*3*2*1. Since there are 3 girls, you can assign them into pairs to sit at the ends in 6 ways. For any given arrangement of two girls at the ends, there are 5 different ways the children in between could sit, so 5! = 120 options. Six different arrangements of 120 options gives 720 ways there could be a girl at each end. So the chance is 720 in 5,040, or 1 in 7.

BRIDGE

Absolutely none. The actual chance of a perfect deal occurring in bridge is 2,235,197,406,985,633,368,301,599, 999 to 1. If the entire population of the planet played 60 hands of bridge every day, newborns included, you'd expect one naturally occurring perfect deal to occur slightly more often than once every 125,000,000,000 years. In practice, shuffling a deck of cards is often done ineffectively, and most occurrences of a perfect deal come down to poor randomization. The rest are the result of deliberate tampering.

THE ENTHUSIAST

The white pieces on the board are in a nearly impossible position. Two bishops of the same colour can never be separated by a single square in a straight line. Well, it is theoretically possible for white to promote a pawn to a second white bishop I suppose, but such a move would be colossally unlikely, particularly in the mid-game. The board must have been set up by a non-player, and the only person with any motive to stage a scene with a game would be the murderer, so Alan Lloyd was the murderer. When faced with his error, Lloyd confessed.

THE FIFTH CAMOUFLAGE

The theme was dining out, and the words were *lay*, *sit*, *eat* and *tip*.

THE RIBBONS

Mrs White. Remembering that each amount spent must be a square number, each mother's length of ribbon must be even, and working through the logic, Daisy bought 4y for 16 pence, and her mother Mrs Green 8y for 64 pence. Rose bought 6y for 36 pence, and her mother Mrs Brown bought 12y for 144 pence. Lily bought 9y for 81 pence and her mother Mrs Black bought 18y for 324 pence. And Heather bought 10y for 100 pence and her mother Mrs White bought 20y for 400 pence.

BILLY AND JONNY

Billy is 30, and Jonny 12. We know $x+y+18=2x$, so $y=x-18$. We also know that $x-y-6=y$, so $2y=x-6$. Substitute through, and $2x-30=x-6$, so $x=30$, and thus $y=12$.

TROUT

72 ounces. If the tail weighs 9, the head must weigh $9+x/2$, and the body, $x = 18+x/2$. So half $x = 18$, and $x=36$, which means the head = 27, and the total is $9+27+36$.

GETTING TO MARKET

10 miles. After 20 minutes, we had travelled half as far as the distance from that spot to Doglick, so it took an hour to Doglick. Then, five miles past Doglick, we had half that 5-mile distance still to go, and that took one hour. So we did 5 miles in 2 hours, our total journey time was 4 hours, and the full distance was 10 miles.

THE TENTH WORDKNOT

The words are *abacterial*, *biocenosis* and *halophytes*, and their broad theme is biology.

PENCILS

By arranging them in alternating rows of 19 and 20, as it turns out. By putting the second row in the hollows of the first, and then the third in the hollows of the second, you save enough space to get a ninth row in place. So you would have 180 pencils if all the rows were 20 pencils long, but four of them are one short, giving you 176 – 16 more than 160.

TWO WRONGS

There are 21 separate solutions, but space forbids me from listing them all. 12734 + 12734 = 25468 gives you the smallest sum, and 49306 + 49306 = 98612 the largest, but any of them will do. To solve this, approach the problem with the same sort of logic that was used in the previous puzzle of this sort. For example, R must be either 2W (if R<5) or 2W+1. The same holds true for I being 2R, 2R+1, or, if 2R>9, 2R−10 – where 2R is a maximum of 18, for 2*9. But since I works of 2R, and R works off 2W, I becomes a function of 4W, and since 2I always has to be less than 19, W cannot be more than 4. Besides, if WR was worth more than 49, there would be an extra letter in front of the word "right". Similarly, the O+O = G and G + G = T mean that O also has to be 4 or less. T must always be even, as there is no '1' to carry over from a previous term. The only way the letters W, R, O, N, G can be zero is if the letter before them is worth 5 or more. When you have some limits attached, try assuming a case where, say, O=0, and you will find that the matter quickly unfolds. Keep attacking in this way, and you will arrive at an effective answer.

EASTER SPIRIT

1.5". Volumes of solids that are the same shape vary according to the cube of their relative lengths. So the largest egg has a comparative volume of 27, being 3" in length. So the volumes of the other three eggs have to add to $27 = x^3 + (x+0.5)^3 + (x+1)^3$. *Regula falsi* is probably simpler here than trying to simplify the equation, so try x=1, for 12.375 (or 2.3^3), and x=2 for 50.625 (or 3.7^3), and you'll see that 1 and 2 put you the same distance from the correct answer, so the midpoint between 1 and 2 must be where the volumes sum to 3^3. In other words, x = 1.5 inches.

THREE MEN

The driver is called Smith. To find the answer, it is useful to keep a grid of possible (and impossible) associations to help make the facts clearer. From (1), Mr Robinson lives in Brixton and, associating (5), is not the professor. From (2), Mr Jones is not the professor either, so the professor is Mr Smith. From (5), Mr Smith lives near the conductor, so Mr Smith also lives in Chelsea. That means Mr Jones must live in Tottenham, and from (4), the conductor is called Jones. So from (3), the ticket inspector can only be Robinson, which means that the driver is called Smith.

RUFUS

16 mph. The overall distance to the end of the road in feet is 625 = 5^4, and the end of the dog's running time is when the distance in feet is 81 = 3^4. These quad roots are obviously in the ratio 5:3, so the sum of the two speeds and the difference between the two speeds must be in the ratio of 5:3, and thus the two speeds in the ratio of 4:1. Wiggins walks at 4 mph, so the dog runs at 16 mph.

MANUAL

It is only possible if one cup is inside another, at which point it becomes trivial. So, for example, you could place a penny in one cup, and then two pennies – and the previous cup and its contents – inside a second cup, and then the remaining seven in the third cup. There are many options, but they all boil down to getting the idea that two of the cups must be nested.

THE TYRANT

If I were to split my marbles evenly, 50 in each jar, then the 50/50 chance of getting either jar would keep my odds of survival at precisely 50%. However, if I place one white marble in one jar, and the other 99 marbles in the other, my chances go up to $1/2*1 + 1/2*49/99$, or 74%. This is as good as it gets. Still not a chance I'd take willingly without significant duress, but a lot better than 50%!

THE FINAL CAMOUFLAGE

The theme was colour, and the words were *ash*, *bole*, ceil and *red*. I was stuck on a theme relating to trees for a long time.

SEVEN APPLEWOMEN

One pricing scheme is 7 apples per penny, until less than 7 remain, at which point the apples become 3 pence per apple. The fact that there are seven women with a maximum number of 140 apples ought to point you towards the divisive break. So the first woman gets 2 pence from 14 apples, plus 18 pence from her remaining 6, whilst the last gets $140/7 = 20$ pence all from batches of 7 apples per penny. The general solution for this sort of puzzle says that for x people with amounts of produce equal to $y(x+0z) + x-1, y(x+1z) + x-2, y(x+2z) + x-3, ...$, then these can be sold at x for 1 penny and then z for each remaining odd item, and all will receive $y + z(x-1)$ pennies. In our case, y, an indeterminate factor in the equation, is equal to 2, giving us a z of 3 for the x of 7.

TERMINUS

The victim's jumper was back to front as well as inside out. One would only have seen the label if standing in front of the man. Bligh claims to have seen the label as the victim ran away, which is impossible, and marks him as the killer.